SUDAN TALES

'These recollections of some Sudan Political Service wives', writes A.R. Walmsley in his foreword, 'touch not only on the horrors but also on the compensations which made their experience so rewarding, above all the camaraderie of the Service and the sterling qualities of the Sudanese people. This is no ordinary history, but an absorbing account of everyday things in a world which has now disappeared where, for fifty years, labouring in extreme conditions, a tiny foreign élite could run a vast country in preparation for its independence.'

Reminiscences of British wives in Sudan between 1926–56 narrated in this collective work encompass the hectic, tragic, adventurous, and above all the comedy of women capable of enduring what cannot be cured. 'Once, while waiting for my husband to appear for lunch at 2.30, I glanced across at our water jug. A very large rat was standing on its hind legs, freely lapping. On B.'s return I said, "I'm afraid I can't stay married to anyone who has rats drinking his drinking water. I am leaving you." B. replied, "How actually will you leave?" Lacking a camel or any other practical transport to the railhead five hundred miles away, that put a stop to the conversation.'

✳

ROSEMARY KENRICK, wife of the former Assistant Adviser to the Governor-General on Constitutional and External Affairs, lived as a Sudan Political Service wife in Talodi (1945–6), Rashad (1946–9), Omdurman (1949–53), and Khartoum (1953–5).

✳

SUDAN TALES

Recollections of some
Sudan Political Service wives
1926–56

∽

compiled by
Rosemary Kenrick

The Oleander Press
17 Stansgate Avenue
Cambridge CB2 2QZ
England

The Oleander Press
210 Fifth Avenue
New York, N.Y. 10010
U.S.A.

British Library Cataloguing in Publication Data
Sudan Tales: recollections of Sudan
   political service wives, 1926–56.
   1. Sudan—Social life and customs
   I. Kenrick, Rosemary
   962.4′03′0922   DT156.7

   ISBN 0–906672–31–7
   ISBN 0–906672–32–5 Pbk

Typeset, printed and bound in Great Britain

Contents

SUDAN TALES

How the Sudan Political Service arose, from military rule. A small band, inevitably élite, administering vast country. Regulations about early marriage.

Wives arriving in 1920s and 1930s. Lack of help and advice. Clothing. Frustration. Egyptian Customs. Heat. Isolation.

Military traditions, wife's illicit arrival; odd rules. Wives still on sufferance – of no use for polo or cricket. Social hierarchy.

Conversation of men at first incomprehensible, Arabic words and local jargon. Importance horses, lions, old boy net. Dependence on conversation, raconteurs and visitors. Still mainly all male company. Wives' interests.

Long and difficult family separations. Sacrifices made to reunite. The Italian threat. War work. Concessions gained. End of pomp and circumstance.

Wives now remaining longer. Arriving in Southern Sudan, living conditions still primitive, concrete square for bath.

Acknowledgements

Without the original idea of Persis Aglen and her continued encouragement, and without the individual accounts supplied by the contributing wives, this book would not have been written. The collective record has produced a fair impression, free of the bias of an individual memoir. Each of these wives deserves credit, as well as my grateful thanks.

I owe an unpayable debt of gratitude to Robert Walmsley for his unfailing and knowledgeable help throughout; never has advice or criticism been more diplomatically couched.

I was fortunate to have the willing cooperation of Bridget Acland, who drew the vignettes; of Cicely Bloss, who generously allowed the use of some of her late husband's photographs; and of Sally Lumley, Broad Oak Studios, who kindly produced the maps.

❅

Illustrations

Unless marked with an asterisk, all photographs were taken by the late
J.F.E. Bloss, MRCS, LRCP, DPH, DRM&H, an Associate of the Royal
Photographic Society, who joined the Sudan Medical Service in 1935.
Showing the country and peoples of Sudan as they were thirty to fifty
years ago, the photographs are reproduced by kind permission of
Cicely Bloss.

Foreword

Interest in our last years of Empire is growing, if we may judge by the recent upsurge of publications about the Indian Raj. It is not only the events in the drama which hold our attention, but more especially the men and women who were actors in it.

Sudan offers a study no less fascinating than India, and it is none too soon to place on record some aspects of a scene on which the curtain fell some thirty years ago. Memories of that time were already fading when I was serving in the Embassy in Khartoum only eight years later, though they were still cherished by many of the Sudanese themselves. Now, the band of those who remember is inevitably reduced.

Rosemary Kenrick, who herself spent many years in Sudan, has performed a notable service in putting together what may respectfully be termed a wives'-eye view. Leaving aside such things as policy and administration, she tells us what was happening on the ground. The sober truth, if sometimes grim, is often hilarious, especially in retrospect.

The men of the Sudan Political Service, a dedicated band addicted to economy and impervious to discomfort, spent much of their lives on trek, and when they were at base they seemed to regard their rather primitive living-quarters as a superior form of tent. Husbands were therefore not the least of the obstacles facing their wives, who struggled to establish something resembling a home, in surroundings which lacked almost everything we take for granted, in searing heat or torrential rains, some hundreds of miles from help or from a neighbour.

These recollections of some Sudan Political Service wives touch not only on the horrors but also on the compensations which made their experience so rewarding, above all the camaraderie of the Service and the sterling qualities of the Sudanese people.

This is no ordinary history, but an absorbing account of everyday things in a world which has now disappeared where, for fifty years, labouring in extreme conditions, a tiny foreign élite could run a vast country in preparation for its independence.

The reader will surely feel not only gratitude to the author and her many sources, but a profound admiration for the administrators of that time and for their indomitable wives; also, not least, affection for the Sudanese.

A.R. WALMSLEY, C.M.G., M.B.E.
Political Counsellor in the
British Embassy, Khartoum. 1963–65

✳

Brief Chronology of Sudan's Modern History

1821 – 1885 Sudan under Turco-Egyptian rule
1881   Muhammad Ahmad ibn Abdallah proclaimed Mahdi
1884   Khartoum under siege
1885   Fall of Khartoum
1885 – 1898 Mahdia
1885   June: death of Mahdi, succeeded by Khalifa Abdullahi
1898   Sept: Khalifa defeated at battle of Karari (Omdurman)
1899   Khalifa killed
1899 – 1955 Anglo-Egyptian Condominium
1899   Anglo-Egyptian Condominium Agreement
1902   Gordon Memorial College opened as secondary school in Khartoum; Grand Hotel built by syndicate
1905   Ten thousand trees planted in Khartoum; work started on Port Sudan
1908 – 10 Blue Nile bridge built between Khartoum and Khartoum North
1911   First girls' elementary school opened at Rufaa
1916   Death of Sultan Ali Dinar; Darfur annexed
1919   Agreement with Plantation Syndicate on Gezira Scheme
1920   Teacher Training College for girls established in Omdurman
1924   Sir Lee Stack murdered in Cairo; Kitchener School of Medicine founded
1925   Midwifery School opened in Omdurman; Sennar dam completed across Blue Nile
1928   Unity High School for girls established by Church Missionary Society in Khartoum
1936   Jebel Aulia dam over White Nile completed
1938   Graduates Congress formed
1940   Kassala occupied by Italians
1941   Kassala won back; Battle of Keren, Eritrea; local government councils established
1942   Graduates Congress memorandum on future of country
1944   Advisory Council of Northern Sudan; Sudan Women's Association formed

1946   First girl went to Gordon Memorial College
1948   Legislative Assembly established; Executive Council formed
1950   Gezira Board formed
1951   Gordon Memorial College combined with Kitchener School of Medicine and became University College of Khartoum; Egypt declared Farouk King of Egypt and Sudan
1952   Farouk deposed by General Neguib in *coup d'état*
1953   Sudanisation Committee established; First elections
1954   Sayid Isma'il el Azhari appointed Prime Minister of first Parliament
1955   Declaration of Independence; gradual departure of Sudan Political Service
1956   **Independence Day,** 1 January

✳

How Britain became Involved

The story of Gordon of Khartoum is now a national legend. However, it does not explain how the vast country of Sudan came to be, in effect, administered by a handful of British for nearly sixty years. Several seemingly unrelated factors led to the British presence in that country. The first and probably most important was the British interest in Egypt.

As soon as the Suez Canal was opened in 1869, the stability of Egypt became of great importance to Britain. Both she and France lent considerable sums of money to bolster the economy of the country. In spite of this Egypt was deemed to be bankrupt in 1881. This led to riots and unrest and the British moved in to restore order and reorganise the country's finances.

When the British High Commissioner in Cairo heard that Turco-Egyptian garrisons in Sudan were being attacked by the local Mahdists, he ordered the evacuation of all troops, and the abandonment of the country, with the exception of the ports. The man appointed to carry out this withdrawal was General Charles Gordon who, some years

Cataracts on the Nile that make navigation south of Wadi Halfa difficult

Remains of Kitchener's 1896 railway

Scrub desert northeast of Atbara

before, had been employed by the Egyptian Khedive as Governor-General of Sudan. For various reasons, some his own, Gordon decided to remain in beleaguered Khartoum instead of retreating. When the Mahdists finally overran the capital in 1885, Gordon was killed. The British government was blamed for not sending aid in time. Gordon was admired by the British public not only for his heroism and his religious faith, but also because he had earlier spent many years trying to suppress the cruel slave-trade which had flourished under Turco—Egyptian rule. The British Government's decision, taken some ten years later in 1896, to send an Expeditionary Force to Sudan was a popular move at home because of the still—remembered circumstances of Gordon's death. A more important factor as far as the government was concerned was the necessity to defend Egypt's southern border against the Mahdist forces who had been constantly attacking it. Lastly there was the urgent need to secure the British stake in the European partition of Africa which was taking place around Sudan's southern borders. Kenya for instance had been declared a British Protectorate only the year before, in 1895.

For all these reasons the Anglo-Egyptian Expeditionary Force set forth from Egypt and by the end of 1896 had occupied Dongola and the Northern Province, thus safeguarding the Egyptian frontier. During those months, attempts to navigate the river south of Wadi Halfa had proved laboriously difficult because of the cataracts, so General Kitchener decided to bypass this whole loop of the Nile and make a direct link to Abu Hamed across two hundred miles of uncharted desert, a daring project whose accomplishment was to be praised by many a government official in the years to come.

From Abu Hamed the two armies continued their slow advance southwards to Khartoum, laying the railway beside the Nile as they went. There were various minor skirmishes on the way, but the main Mahdist forces were not defeated until the famous battle of Omdurman, in September 1898. According to an officer present at the time, Kitchener then crossed the Nile two days later and landed outside Gordon's ruined palace in Khartoum. There two flagstaffs were erected; the Union Jack was run up one as the National Anthem was played; then the green Egyptian flag was run up the other, to the accompaniment of the Egyptian National Anthem. This was the first outward and visible sign of the Prime Minister, Lord Salisbury's original firm intention not to annex the Sudan as a colony, but to govern the country as a condominium under joint trusteeship. On 19 January the following year, 1898, the two governments signed the agreement and the Condominium of the Anglo-Egyptian Sudan was proclaimed. This cumbersome name was retained only for official use and the country continued to be called, as in Arabic, 'as-Sudan', 'the Sudan'.

1 *The Service they Married*

Although knowledge of the Indian Civil Service is fairly widespread, fewer people know about the Sudan Political Service, or indeed about the country itself. For this reason this book includes a short chronology of Sudan's modern history, and a brief account of how Britain became involved.

The Condominium of the Anglo-Egyptian Sudan was established when the Anglo-Egyptian Expeditionary Force re-occupied Sudan in 1899. The various provinces in the country were therefore initially administered by British officers of the Egyptian Army helped by Egyptian Mamurs (administrative officers). The War Office in London had a habit of recalling officers unexpectedly, as for example on the outbreak of the Boer War so, in an endeavour to maintain continuity, it was decided to introduce a civilian element. The first six civilians were recruited in 1901, and from then on an average of eight probationers joined this administrative service each year. They wore the same uniform as the British officers of the Egyptian Army but were distinguished (as were the rest of the departmental staff) by wearing a blue puggaree round their pith helmet. Some time after the 1914–18 war this small civilian cadre became known as 'political' to differentiate them from the other civilians in government service.

In 1924 the unexpected murder in Cairo of the Governor-General Sir Lee Stack forced a change in regime. Egyptian officers returned to Egypt, the Sudan Defence Force came into existence and the administration became entirely civilian. British officers wishing to serve the Sudan Government retired from the Army.

Who were these first civilian members of the Sudan Political Service and how had they been selected? Lord Cromer, still 'the all-powerful

1

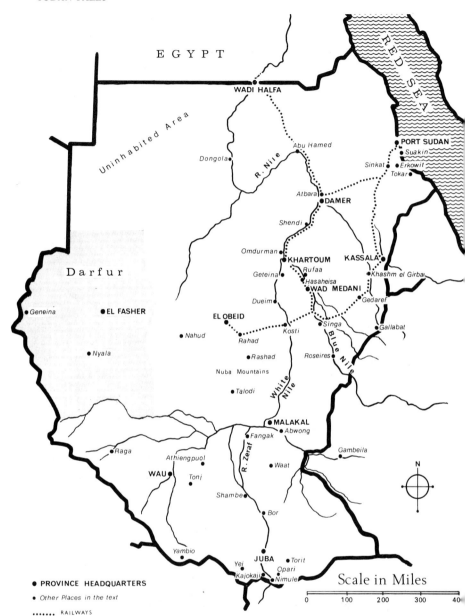

The ANGLO-EGYPTIAN SUDAN

representative of the British Government in Egypt', had decreed at the outset that 'active young men, endowed with good health, high character and fair abilities' should be recruited.

'Good health' meant that they must be tough enough to withstand several bouts of malaria a year and to survive the ensuing and often fatal black-water fever. 'High character' meant that they must be prepared to face separation from their family – if they were foolish enough to have one – and also to be able to administer virtually on their own a district the size of Wales, in searing heat and harsh conditions. 'Fair abilities' meant that they must be capable of passing both the necessary law and Arabic exams within the first two years.

Candidates were selected from universities by interview and not by examination. It is irreverent, but not irrelevant in a country without other forms of entertainment, to recall that 'Do you play bridge?' was one of the questions often asked.

Three of the conditions of service laid down were that because of the appalling climate no one had to spend more than nine months in any one year in the country; that they had to retire at or before fifty; and that no member of the service could marry until he had been out for four years (at some time between the two wars this was reduced to two years, or until the age of twenty-seven had been reached.) There was at the time nothing surprising in this edict: a similar one was imposed by the Army. In their headquarters in Khartoum hung a framed undertaking signed by none other than Field-Marshal Haig himself, that he would resign his commission before becoming either engaged or married. One reason for the restriction was the absence of medical facilities for wives in the out-stations where juniors were likely to be posted.

Selection on Lord Cromer's criteria resulted in a corps of dedicated men. Duty and uncomplaining endurance remained tenets of their faith. Admittedly, out in the wild, be it desert, scrub or swamp, there existed few distractions. In some cases ambition fuelled ceaseless work, but in general the only reward lay in personal satisfaction. Most members of the Political Service came to have a genuine interest in, and affection for, whatever tribe they happened to have been asked to administer, championing it and vindicating it in any dispute. As Colonel John Orlebar mentions in his *Tales of the Sudan Defence Force*, these attitudes were admired by his officers when they were on military patrols together in the late 1920s; and various people who came to the country after World War II, on whatever pretext, were also complimentary, as for example Sir Laurence Grafftey–Smith, a member of the Governor-General's Advisory Commission (*Hands to Play*, p.164)

In its brief existence of some fifty-seven years, the total British element within the Sudan Political Service reached only 393. This figure must be seen against the vast extent of the Sudan, larger than the combined territories of the E.E.C., peopled by five hundred and ninety-seven extremely diverse tribes. Some 40% of the population, in the 1950s, claimed membership of an Arab tribe, and Arabic was the *lingua franca* of the north; but in the south there were the confusingly numerous tribes of the Nilotic, Nilo-Hamitic and Sudanic groups, among whom only a rudimentary Arabic was spoken and where English consequently became the official language. There was a total religious and cultural divide between the rigidly Muslim north and the rest of Sudan, where a great variety of pagan beliefs held sway, mingled later with Christianity. Many other British officials worked in many other departments, all concerned with the administration of the country but, even so, the numbers of the Sudan Political Service were by any reckoning modest indeed.

It is interesting to see the sources from which it was recruited in the following table compiled by R.C. Mayall, the Sudan Agent in London 1941-51, which appeared in the Sudan Political Service list published in the 1950s.

Years	Oxford University		Cambridge University		Others (e.g. Soldiers, other Universities, etc.)		Total
1899–1914	...	37	...	23	...	28	...	88
1915–1933	...	89	...	43	...	53	...	185
1934–1939	...	23	...	15	...	5	...	43
1941–1944	...	4	...	1	...	3	...	8
1945–1951	...	29	...	21	...	19	...	69
TOTAL	...	182	...	103	...	108	...	393

A Sudan Defence Force band

Dinka homestead on east bank of Nile near Bor

The relatively small number of the Service fostered a certain degree of élitism. As its members, unlike those of the Colonial Service, were not transferred to other countries, they became a remarkably close-knit group, partly because of common interests, and partly because transfers every two or three years within the country encouraged many firm friendships. These elements led to a degree of exclusiveness which did not escape the criticism, or the envy, of other expatriates in the country.

The bond within the group survived dispersal and separation, and at subsequent reunions members quickly and easily resumed their former cordial familiarity: indeed, since the Service disbanded in 1956, members have continued to keep in close touch, unless or until death hath them parted.

❋

5

2 First time out – Pre-War

Not many wives coming out to Sudan before the last War would previously have even crossed the Channel. It is difficult today to remember how comparatively rare and restricted foreign travel was sixty years ago. Nor, in the days before television, did many wives know exactly where and what 'Sudan' was, apart from the fact that it was in Africa. At school they might have heard of Khartoum in relation to Gordon's death there, but in many minds the country must have been as vaguely fixed on the map as the often-mentioned Timbuktu. ('*The* Sudan' is correct and represents the Arabic name of the country, but in deference to modern English usage 'Sudan' will henceforth generally be used, except in quotations).

Before air travel, wives had the choice of two routes from England to Sudan. The shorter way involved landing in Egypt, taking the night train from Cairo to Shellal, then boarding the Nile steamer to Wadi Halfa. The longer trip, usually favoured by those burdened with much baggage, was through the Suez Canal and down the Red Sea to the country's only port, laconically if unimaginatively called Port Sudan. (Before the port was opened in 1909 there had been a small Arab settlement on the site known as Marsa Barghout.) From here, as also from Wadi Halfa, a train ran to Khartoum.

Everyone coming to Sudan for the first time admired the trains painted white to reflect the heat. They were the one exception to the Government's overriding principle that economy must come before comfort, for in those days countries lived scrupulously within their budgets. The first-class sleepers on these trains were spacious and comfortable, as a wife recalls: 'Small wash-basins let down from the polished wood interior, there was an electric fan and an armchair. The

6

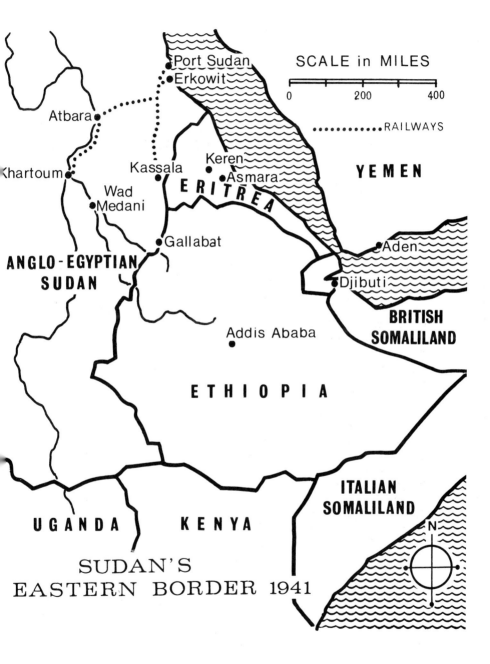

SUDAN'S
EASTERN BORDER 1941

The Nile north of Atbara

Tebeldi trees in the Nuba mountains north of Talodi

large windows had three frames, of tinted glass, mosquito wire and louvred shutters, each of which could be moved up or down independently. In the dining car there were huge electric fans overhead like propeller blades and good meals were efficiently served.' Advantageously as these carriages compared with the best Continental trains, travelling in them between latitude fifteen and twenty-one degrees did much to diminish one's pleasure. With a following wind it could be very hot indeed. One bride did in fact remark on the oppressive heat, 'If you want to enjoy this country,' her husband told her, 'never, ever, mention the heat.' There was a well-known saying that if a bride could stand the thirty-six hour journey from Port Sudan to Khartoum, she would be able to survive the rest of her time in the country.

This first train journey vividly brought home to newcomers the vast size of Sudan. Used to the quickly-changing landscapes of the U.K., they marvelled at travelling for hours through unchanging terrain, be it desolate desert sand or stunted scrub. In that central band of country, small or larger piles of rocks, small or larger hills, rose as abruptly and as inconsequentially as so many coal tips from an otherwise interminably flat plain.

Remembering her first train journey from Port Sudan in 1938 a wife wrote: 'The train moved at little more than ten miles an hour because of the narrow gauge. At first it rumbled along the maritime plain, then with an extra engine chugged up into the Red Sea hills. At some time British regiments stationed at Gebeit had set out their regimental badges in white stones. These stood out well against the grim black

The sudd south of Malakal

9

Gum Arabic at Nyala

rock. After this the train went on through nothing but dull uninterest-
ing desert and scrub'.

The train journey into Khartoum from Wadi Halfa seemed equally
unspectacular. 'Within two minutes of leaving Halfa there was no vegetation at all, just miles and miles of sand and brown hills. At regular
intervals we passed or stopped at watering stations which had no name,
only a number. Each was just a collection of *tukls* (huts) with conical
white roofs. When the train stopped we were able to step down and
walk along the line and I was surprised to see mirages everywhere. I
had thought they were rare and connected to dire thirst and consequent light-headedness.' As this wife soon realised, mirages were
common. A mother, bringing out her daughter of nine for the first
time, was heard to say: 'Do you see that large lake over there? Well, it
isn't there at all'.

Before travelling on this train from Wadi Halfa, wives would have
had to contend with the overland journey through Egypt. On landing
at Alexandria, they first encountered the frustrating nuisance of Egyptian Customs. 'It was to take us two hours' a wife recalls 'to pass through
Customs. For one hour we waited to pay fifteen piastres (15p) quaran-
tine fee. We were sixth in the queue but we never moved forward
because those at the back sent their passports round with a bribe and
were processed first. So when at last we managed to reach the Customs
shed itself, we adopted the same principle. Consequently all our trunks
were marked through to Shellal at once, without any trouble, while
others, more high-minded, had every single item opened'.

With a modicum of luck and the payment of sufficient bribes, passengers could sometimes arrive in Cairo in time to catch the night train south. Newcomers found Cairo station a terrifying chaos of noise and frenzy, which prompted a 1945 bride to write: 'porters rushed at us to snatch our cases all shouting and fighting for possession.' She was thankful that their compartment had been previously reserved for them by the Sudan Agent. When the last of the arguing and innumerable porters had been paid off, she settled back with a sigh of relief as the train drew away from the station.

The arrival at Shellal the next day seemed 'by comparison', the same bride remembers, 'orderly and quiet. We boarded the paddle steamer that was to take us on up the Nile to Wadi Halfa. This was the most perfect form of travel that I have ever experienced. The roomy cabins had beds, running water and were light and airy. Each one opened onto the covered deck where there always seemed to be a welcome breeze. If it became cool towards evening we moved forward to a glassed-in-room in the bow. All the time the banks of the Nile just slipped by. For miles and miles there was nothing at all but sand, with every now and then groups of date palms around little box-like houses with shuttered windows. Sometimes these were painted white or dull red but usually were just mud coloured.'

Another bride coming out that same year has a vivid memory of her first impressions. 'The setting sun turned the rolling sand hills and

Fasher aerodrome

dunes every shade of apricot and salmon, a miraculous kaleidoscope of breathtaking beauty. Having only a black and white film in my camera there was no temptation to try to capture the colour before it all too soon began to fade with oncoming darkness. I could not help but think of Blake's lines.

He who binds to himself a joy
Doth the wingéd life destroy.
But he who kisses the joy as it flies
Lives in Eternity's sunrise.

It was a spectacle I have never forgotten and one that I have not yet seen adequately reproduced on film or photograph.'

This Nile trip, pleasant during the winter months, became less congenial during the summer. 'In May 1940 home leave was stopped so we decided to go to the Lebanon. At Shellal the thermometer in our cabin registered 127°F. Three weeks later, Italy having entered the war, we were instantly recalled. By then it was even hotter and the frame of my bed in the cabin almost too hot to touch'.

These descriptions of the boat trip to and from Shellal are by now historic because in 1955, with the completion of the Aswan High Dam in Egypt, practically the whole one hundred and eighty miles of this stretch of the Nile became the vast Lake Nasser, inundating Wadi Halfa itself, which ceased to exist.

In the early days, the majority of wives coming out to Sudan remained in Khartoum. From 1926 onwards, more of them started to go to Province headquarters, and to out-stations if, and only if, these happened to be either on the Nile or on the railway. So in many of these out-stations they were not only the first white women to be seen but also the first British wives to cope with trekking. They would be unlikely to know any other woman who could give them advice about the kind of life they were likely to lead or the most suitable type of clothes to wear.

A wife who remained in Sudan over the following twenty-seven years records her first experience of the country in 1926.

'When I became engaged I began to read quite a large selection of travellers' tales about the Nile and darkest Africa, all supplied by a local lending library. I was relieved to learn that a considerable number of accompanying 'ladies' (including a Circassian slave, later to become that respectable matron, Lady Baker), had braved the wilds before the 1914-18 war. I knew that several officers' wives had come to Khartoum, with their ladies' maids, soon after the reconquest. But it was all very new to my deaf aunt who told everyone that I was engaged "to a commissionaire in St. Anne's". (Those of us living in the north pronounced 'Sudan' to rhyme with Anne, hence the confusion with the Lancashire town of Lytham St. Anne's).

I had no friends who could give me any advice about clothes, so my mother asked some tropical outfitters. They prescribed non-see-through cotton dresses to avoid wearing a petticcoat, sea island cotton undies, and a dressing gown with matching pyjamas. In those days we wore lisle stockings by day and silk for occasions. The firm advised, and made me, khaki drill jackets with enormouse pockets to wear with either breeches and boots or very long shorts and knee-length socks. Hardly a becoming outfit, but one practical for trek I was told firmly. Equally off-putting were the white thigh-length mosquito boots especially made for me to wear in the evening. I promptly chopped these down to knee-length once I was out there. Considered essential at that time was a double *terai* consisting of two felt hats, one inside the other, which could also be worn separately. I thought mine was very smart; it was blue on top and pinky fawn underneath. Dark glasses were not always worn until after the war. The only toiletries I took were Pond's cold cream, talcum powder and a compact. I can't remember about sanitary towels (Tampax tampons had not been invented then, or I didn't know about them) but I must have taken out at least six months' supply along with candles, saddle soap, Keating's insect powder and tinned fruit.

We were married in July and my husband's leave ended in September. It was thought that both the Red Sea and the Sudan would be too hot for me then and so it was suggested that I wait and travel out with all the other wives in November.

However in the end we managed to travel together. On arrival in Port Sudan I can remember being very disappointed to see Fuzzy-Wuzzies (Hadendowa belonging to the Beja) mundanely unloading our ship. Having read Kipling, as everyone had in those days, I was expecting to see them standing with their long spears, romantically silhouetted against the sky, gazing from the top of the hills into the far distance. I was very impressed with the train and the spacious sleeping compartments but thought the country we passed through very monotonous. At the various halts the humbler third-class passengers ran quickly up to the engine with their tea-pots for some boiling water, or bought sweet drinks and unidentifiable small snacks. We in the first class were only too thankful to be able to clamber down and stretch our legs.

When at last we arrived at Khartoum station we found my husband's servants waiting to meet us. (In fact our telegram had not arrived and they had been meeting every train from Port Sudan for some days.) After greeting them we took a taxi and went to the hotel – what happened to all our baggage and our abandoned stores I don't know; everyone's honesty then was taken for granted. The Grand Hotel really was luxurious in those days, a haven of civilised comfort with its fans, running water, cold baths and iced lemon.

13

There were cheerful, willing servants at every corner. We sat under
the palm trees at the front of the hotel and there, just across the road,
was the Blue Nile flowing by.

We had to spend two or three days in Khartoum and on one of
them we were invited to play golf at Khartoum North with two government officials, one of whom then gave us a wedding present on
behalf of all the province D.C.s. To my amazement it turned out to
be a set of pure silver finger bowls each ornamented with a crocodile
which was the province crest. These had been made by the sil-
versmiths in Omdurman who, in those days, sold their wares comparatively cheaply. One night a fellow Scot, a senior Agricultural
officer, gave us dinner. He was surprisingly forthcoming from the
start although we still addressed each other as 'Mr' and 'Mrs'. He
arranged for us to go round to his office the next morning so that I
could choose a cook as he said it was very important for me to select
one with a face I liked. This I found difficult for all dark faces then
seemed to look alike.

During the three days I was in Khartoum. I spoke to only one
woman and that came about by chance. The province steamer to take
us to Geteina next day had been conveniently moored just outside
the hotel. We were struggling to unpack our cutlery, bedding and so
forth by the light of a dim street lamp and our own hurricane lamp.
The Governor of Khartoum's house was just opposite and he must
have seen us; so he sent a message across asking us in for a drink. I
was surprised to find the Governor and his wife both so unstarchy.
My spirits rose; perhaps I would 'do' after all?

The next morning we set off up the White Nile to Geteina where
we were to stay for the next year or two. My husband had the job of
registering the houses and the riverain cultivations because compen-
satory lots would have to be given once the Jebel Aulia Dam was built.

We finally arrived at Geteina on 4 October at the inconvenient
hour of six p.m. Darkness falls quickly in the Sudan and there is very
little twilight. We had to be carried ashore as the Nile was at its post-
rains height. All our gear had to be put ashore in the dark as the province steamer was needed at Dueim the next morning. I suppose we
had some kind of meal that evening but I can only remember the
climb up the steep steps to the bathroom roof and lying on our 'an-
qaraybs (native beds) under the glorious starry sky. Later we used to
take up a chart to try to trace the various constellations.

Next morning my husband left for the office. It never occurred to
either of us that he should have the morning off for domestic
reasons. I don't remember being at all afraid at being left on my own.
I suppose I was conditioned at all costs, not to be 'silly'.

I had learnt some Arabic at Manchester University using

14

Thatcher's Arabic grammar – so I could decline a verb and understand about broken plurals, quite useless at this stage, but a blessing later on. The servants and I got on somehow.

There was no Greek merchant in Geteina and ordering goods from Khartoum was a lengthy business and expensive too, as everything had to come down on the fortnightly post boat. There were local traders and a *suq* on Fridays.

With so many effective insecticides available today, it is extraordinary to remember that our only recourse against plagues of all sorts then were Jeyes' fluid, Lifebuoy soap and Keating's powder. A fly swat had to be carried at all times; some horsy types had a switch of horsehair on a polished baton. The arrival a year or two later of the 'Flit-gun', a cumbersome tin sprayer, proved an immense boon.

I don't quite know what I did all morning. I planned some shelves and cupboards to be made out of our packing cases, and made some curtains with material I had bought in England. These were all sewn by hand as I did not own a sewing machine till later. I remember playing patience and of course I tried to do some Arabic exercises by myself. Unfortunately there was no one who spoke English who could correct them or with whom I could practise speaking. The house was very hot and I only had my own small fan so I expect I dozed a lot, as most people did in their first year before they had become used to the climate.

In the early morning I would ride with my husband and in the cool weather I would often go out again after breakfast on my own. Frequently I walked along the river shore, for every day it changed and I was interested in the wild flowers.'

The first Flora of the Sudan was not published until 1929 and this wife would not at this time have had the advantage of a copy of Grace Crowfoot's illustrated *Flowering Plants of North and Central Sudan* (1928) based on her botanical drawings made between 1905-25. Although her book contained no fewer than sixteen different Acacias, it covered only a fraction of the families and species. The first volume of an official Sudan Flora did not appear until 1949.

While walking or riding beside the White Nile this wife also noticed 'thousands of water birds. But sadly', she continued, 'I never learned about them.' Without any previous ornithological knowledge it was almost impossible to make much progress. An illustrated book on South African birds became available only after the War, and Cave and MacDonald's excellent, definitive *Birds of the Sudan* was published only in 1955, sadly on the very eve of most wives' departure.

Lacking in 1926 both these aids, which could have made her life more interesting, this particular wife yet gives the impression that she

15

was luckily intelligent enough to be able to rely on her own resources. In fact, in this ability lay one key, the other being good health, to enjoying rather than disliking the country. She appeared reluctant then, as she still is today, to admit publicly that her life in Geteina could have been less than perfect, rather like the attitude of another young bride, who came out the following year and whose first station was Talodi in the Nuba Mountains. As this was then a Province headquarters, besides the Governor, there were the Deputy, two British military officers and a manager of the cotton ginnery, all bachelors except for the Governor, whose wife the new girl unfortunately found 'rather forbidding'. This was the least of her troubles because as she admits, 'I had always been allergic to all flying creatures including birds, so what I hated most on arrival were all the moths and "sausage flies" that flew into my hair when the lamps were lit in the evenings. But I decided that if I were to go on living in the country then somehow I must overcome my phobia. There were some terrible evenings of agony but eventually I won through.'

In those early years the wives of junior members of the service, who were often the first women to come to out-stations, felt they were on approval and would be sent back, as it were from the front, if unsatisfactory. For this reason they determined not to complain. 'No one today can believe what women put up with in the Sudan in the 'thirties. Liberated? – we were barely tolerated.'

In 1928 a young wife came out to the country for the first time to join her husband, as she thought, in his house at Abwong, east of Malakal, Upper Nile Province. On reaching the province headquarters in Malakal, she was told that he was out on a military patrol and that she must travel on southwards up the Nile.

'I was feeling very forlorn as I had had to leave my baby daughter behind in order to join my husband. In Malakal I was told that I would have to go further on up the Nile to the small village of Bor to stay with the Russian wife of another D.C. who was out on patrol with my husband. Bor, completely isolated in the *Sudd*, was at this moment flooded in all directions as the rains had started. The two of us were completely alone, our only callers being a well-known herd of elephants three hundred strong. The bungalow in which we lived was the home of many undisturbed mice and rats. Often we felt movements under the cushions on which we were sitting and discovered that it was mice enjoying the kapok filling.

It was all very novel to me as I had come straight from Mayfair and fashion-designing. In spite of the humidity I found it fascinating but the time difficult to fill. I soon took out my paint box to sketch. We were surrounded by tall Dinka and Nuer cattle owners, who would stand for long spells on one foot, the sun shining on their muscular

EGYPT

Uninhabited Area

NORTHERN

RED SEA

PORT SUDAN

KASSALA

DAMER

KHARTOUM
KHARTOUM

KASSALA

WAD MEDANI

DARFUR

EL FASHER

KORDOFAN

EL OBEID

BLUE
NILE

BAHR
el GHAZAL

WAU

MALAKAL

UPPER
NILE

N

WAU

EQUATORIA

JUBA

Scale in Miles

0   100   200   300   400

• PROVINCE HEADQUARTERS

PROVINCES in the
ANGLO-EGYPTIAN SUDAN   1945

17

The main canal in the Gezira with the Blue Nile beyond

bodies. They had ornamental hair styles and the young warriors carried two spears, one specifically for fish hunting. They did not like me looking straight at them so I had to be careful and do my sketches by stealth.

Our two husbands were out trying to find a witch-doctor, Gwek Wonding, who had incited some of his tribe to murder their D.C.' Captain Fergusson, together with a Greek merchant and sixteen Dinka porters, had been killed by Nuer at Lake Jur on 14 December 1927. Nuer and Dinka were always fighting. There were patrols on both sides of the Nile during 1928.

'These rebels then started to build an enormous earth pyramid, Deng Kur, as a memorial. Eventually the trouble-makers were rounded up and tried. We were overjoyed when at last our husbands were able to return.

It was decreed that one of the trouble-makers should be hanged. This had to happen in his own village to be an example; so we were given a lorry and set out with only vague directions to find the place. At some points the condemned man, in chains, had to walk in front to show us the best way. This did not seem particularly strange in such a remote wild place. At last we reached the village and the gallows which had been sticking through the cab window on the journey were removed and erected. I heard the hammering for hours.

Next morning my husband got up very early and in the dawn silence there was just the sound of natives walking to the site. It was very eerie. Then there was a great shout. The bull terrier started howling and rushed under my camp bed. The end had come. Both men came back looking very shaken. I sat them down at once to their breakfast with their backs to the poor swinging man. There seemed to be no hard feelings and almost immediately other chiefs came up for a chat. However I was thankful to be off and away. It was a long and uncomfortable trek back in the heat and the lorry had to be dug out several times.'

Gwek Wonding was killed in an attack near his pyramid on 1 February 1929.

Later on her husband was transferred to Nahud in Kordofan, 'an oasis of white buildings and palms, where the exciting Friday market was a wonderful sight of colour and movement, everyone getting in everyone's way. There were assorted bundles of hides, large piles of gum arabic (waiting to be exported to Rowntree's for their fruit gums) and camels walking over merchants' carpets, rolled up or on display.' She then goes on to admit that, much as she enjoyed the life here, 'it had been a hundred times more exciting in the south even though it had been more primitive.'

An artist, this wife easily recaptured visual scenes and like many other wives found recalling incidents relatively easy. But very rarely indeed did any of the contributors write about their emotions. No-one, man or woman, could have escaped being assailed, while on their first tour, by 'the blues', that appalling desolation of home-sickness. Yet this has not been mentioned by anyone, maybe partly because these early wives belonged to a generation brought up to suppress, rather than express, any emotions, 'keeping a stiff upper lip'. Secondly, in the course of thirty years or more, the sharpest feelings have been covered with sand. Wives have tended as a defence to mask with attempted humour any dismay they might have felt at the time.

❋

3 *The Military Legacy*

Because the early members of the Political Service worked alongside the officers of the Egyptian Army they wore the same uniform. But after 1925 the army uniform was worn on official occasions only, and for everyday wear an army-type bush jacket and shorts came into use. Gold braid was still retained on the shoulder tabs to denote rank and juniors continued, for many years to come, the habit of saluting their seniors.

The hierarchy of the Political Service had a certain similarity to that of the army, as originally the Province Governor had also been Commanding Officer. When, in 1925, he became a civilian his second-in-command was called Deputy Governor. Together they administered that particular province with the help of six or seven District Commissioners and a similar number of Assistant District Commissioners (confusingly called A.D.C.s). The lowest cadre of the British administration was the new boy who remained a Probationer until he had passed the necessary exams. The exact number of provinces varied over the years owing to periodic splitting or amalgamation. In 1955 there were eight provinces and two commissionerships (Khartoum and Port Sudan).

For most of the year social life in any province headquarters would have been all male and similar to that in any army mess. In out-stations junior members lived as if on manoeuvres and knew they could not marry until they had been in the country some years. An early engagement was also discouraged. One young man, who had become engaged during his leave in 1925, was told on his return to Sudan by his superior that 'he had made a very grave mistake.' Authority tried to deter another Probationer. 'We actually married before we should, for although my husband had been out for two years, his appointment had not quite been confirmed. On our honeymoon we received a telegram from the Civil Secretary's Office saying "Strongly advise you not to marry". Of course I was not allowed to go out with my husband that year but I did the next.' A year later in 1928 another fiancée had her expected engagement of six months greatly prolonged. 'My husband had taken very late leave that year in order to hunt. After we became engaged his Governor in Kordofan promised he could have early leave the following Spring in order to come back to marry me.' News of this proposed plan must have reached the Civil Secretary's Office for 'just before he left England he quite unexpectedly heard that he had been transferred to Raga near the south-western border. This out-station, just about as far from Khartoum as you could go, lay in a District where no wife could reside without special official permission. So we had to wait twenty months before we could marry.'

During the early 1930s another fiancée, recently down from Cambridge, was not so acquiescent.

'It seemed inconceivable that any rule should be laid down about when and if a person could marry. It was possible to understand one of the reasons given – that a man needed some time on his own to learn such a demanding job. Also a young A.D.C. might be posted to a place which would not be suitable for his wife. This seemed a fair reason for not allowing his wife to join him; she might upset the whole local administration by becoming frequently and seriously ill with malaria, dysentery, bilharzia, or anything else, or by complaining about the conditions to such an extent that her husband could not concentrate on his work. But why only in the first year? It could happen at any time. It did not seem a valid reason against getting married; which is what we did.'

This illicit marriage had a sequel. It so happened that the husband was stationed within reach of Wadi Halfa, just inside the Sudan border with Egypt, and that he became entitled to one week's leave.

'For the sake of this one possible week together I travelled out to Egypt by train and ship in the winter of 1934-35, and by train and river steamer to Wadi Halfa. On the station platform in Cairo, never having set foot in Egypt or indeed Africa before, I began to feel not a little lost. A kind man came up and asked if he could help. I explained the situation at unnecessary length. That I was married to a member of the Sudan Political Service but that we ought not to be married; that I ought not to be going to the Sudan at all but that I was going; that a week's leave could be taken, though not strictly in Egypt on the very edge; and that it would be idiotic if any of the Sudanese authorities took the slightest notice of this. Having listened patiently, he said "You have told the wrong person – I am the Sudan Agent in Cairo". He then looked suddenly amused, shrugged his shoulders and left it at that.'

It was not until the following autumn that this wife could officially enter the Sudan.

Even when their arrival was legitimate, these early wives found themselves, in places other than Khartoum, very much alone in a man's world. They realised, or were made to realise by bachelor officials, that they constituted a nuisance, a liability, and were there on sufferance, because government officials of all departments had become accustomed to working and living in a male society – and some liked to keep it this way.

In Sir Harold MacMichael's book, *The Anglo-Egyptian Sudan,* published in 1934, there is not one mention of a British woman from start to finish. (The name of the hospital ship on the Upper Nile, *The Lady Baker,* doesn't count because this lady was not originally British.) In his second excellent book, published in 1954, 'men and women' missionaries get a mention on page 139 but not specifically British ones; they could have been Italian, Australian or American. If by chance one sentence on page 127 were skipped, the reader would gain the impression that there neither had been, nor were, any British women in the country – no teachers, no nurses, no doctors and certainly no mere wives.

The wives were a liability because the utterly dedicated senior officials felt they might deflect the single-minded devotion which was expected from, and given by, junior members of the Service. Authority erred in this fear: any call from the local population took and continued to take immediate and easy precedence over any previously-arranged domestic commitment.

Finally, wives would be a nuisance because they were sure to be 'silly' or to complain – and anyway they were of no use for either the polo or the cricket team.

Consequently during the late 1920s any wives out in the Sudan soon learned that if they were seen at least they should not be heard. 'I was surprised to find that both sheep and goats were browny black and so, from a distance, difficult to distinguish. At one of the halts on my first train journey I announced with triumph that I could now tell the difference because the tails of the goats turned up while the longer tails of the sheep hung down. My husband frowned at me because I had spoken rather loudly (or he thought I had) and had shown up my ignorance in front of other passengers. It is impossible to realise now, fifty years later, how naive and anxious to please "the powers that be" new wives of my type were.'

Another husband evidently thought that wives should not even be seen. Returning from leave by train, he off-loaded his bride at the previous small halt because he anticipated a royal welcome for her at the

Ferry boat south of Wadi Halfa

main station, Um Ruaba. He did not think it right (only in Muslim eyes?) for his wife to be made a fuss of. His decision might well have been influenced by the prevalent Muslim outlook. The firm policy of the Sudan Political Service required respect for, and non-interference with, local customs and attitudes, provided that these did not contravene the Penal Code. The low and inferior state of Muslim women had not altered since Biblical days, when men regarded them as chattels along with 'his ox or his ass or anything that is his'.

A local shaikh was once escorting the D.C. and his wife on a tour of inspection round a remote corner of the district. At a certain point it was found that one too few horses had been provided for the party. '*Malaysh* (Never mind)' said the shaikh firmly, if hopefully, 'we can leave the *sitt* (lady) behind.'

Wives in the 1920s meeting with opposition both before and after arriving needed to be determined to put up with almost anything during the few months they could be with their husbands. This stoic acceptance and uncomplaining attitude was to be emulated by the majority of wives who followed them; but by the 'thirties some of them began to be more critical, and not always silently so. 'So many rules and regulations were issued to wives,' complained a wife sharply, arriving in Darfur in 1935, 'in some ways we seemed to be back at school. I began to wonder whether all these impressive representatives of our country had ever really grown up.' One of their number, Reginald Davies, parodied the situation with the self-mockery characteristic of the Service.

A Bride's Welcome to Darfur

The Governor said, "I will have her to stay
To instruct her on how to behave,
As to when to be silent and when she may speak,
(If shop talk for one moment I waive.)

How lucky she is, though as yet unaware,
To have ME to ensure she won't stumble.
If attentive, she'll turn out a good D.C's wife,
Unobtrusive and thrifty and humble."

It should be explained that Darfur Province during the nineteen-twenties and 'thirties had some notoriously and exceptionally autocratic governors. Perhaps this was partly due to the fact that the Governor resided in the former palace of Sultan Ali Dinar in El Fasher. One wife remembers this as 'an imposing white-washed, castellated building, approached up wide steps, at the foot of which on either side were two small cannons. The atmosphere was feudal. On arrival we were informed that no one however senior could wear a blue shirt until he had been in the Province for two years. Such an absurd rule – our reaction was unprintable.' But at that time, 1934, it was not 'so absurd'. A similar edict existed in a certain public school in England then, that no new boy should put his hands in his pockets until he had been at the school for two years. In spite of the rigours of the climate this rule was uncomplainingly adhered to. One of the victims, recalling the custom today, did not even think it odd. There was another instance of the prefect-fag relationship when a young D.C. was transferred from Wau, in the south, in 1938. He and his wife thought they were going to Kassala so travelled to Kosti by lorry and steamer. On arrival they were told to go to Darfur instead and this meant catching the train for El Obeid. The wife continues. 'We duly arrived on Christmas Eve. As we had been travelling for so long already, we decided to spend Christmas Day resting in El Obeid before tackling the arduous four-day lorry trip to El Fasher. As a result of this my husband was under a cloud for some time as he had not had permission from the Governor of Darfur to spend an extra night en route.' The wives tended to be more rebellious about these strictures than their husbands; but then they stayed in the country only for a short time and their career was not at stake.

It was not only junior members of the Service who were treated in this autocratic fashion. During the war, one Governor of Darfur wired the U.S. Air Force that they could not land at the particular time they requested as he would be playing polo that afternoon on the landing strip. This could be interpreted as arrogance but, as Jarvis wickedly wrote about the British Army in Egypt on page 75 of *Oriental Spotlight*, 'In these highly mechanised days it is so perfectly obvious that the finest – in fact, the only – training for actual warfare is polo...' He based this comment on the amount of polo played at the Gezira Club in Cairo. However the ability to play polo became so important in Darfur that it often dictated who was to be transferred there.

Polo, certainly another military legacy, was played wherever two teams could be mustered. At one time in the Blue Nile Province, because of the Gezira Cotton Syndicate staff, enough Old Etonians could be found to make a whole team. The opposition called themselves the Borstal Boys.

In parenthesis, here, the Gezira cotton scheme should be explained. From very early days the Sudan Government determined to increase the almost non-existent revenue of the country by growing cotton commercially. In 1904 a vast triangular island (gezira) of black, unendingly flat soil between the two Niles, south of Khartoum, had been designated as a suitable area for cotton growing. Unfortunately, the unreliable rainfall meant that irrigation on a large scale would be needed, but no funds existed. So initially various smaller projects were started in other areas which could make use of flood water. After the 1914-18 war the British Government were persuaded to put up the money for the much needed dam at Sennar on the Blue Nile. It opened in 1926. The Sudan Government decreed that they, and the indigenous settled tenant-landowners, would each have 40% of the profits. The Sudan Plantation Syndicate, designated to run the scheme, would use the remaining 20% for administration and research. This admirable scheme was extremely well run. By 1950 an unbelievable three-thousand five hundred miles of canal had been dug, and the Government were receiving an annual revenue of about £16m., representing three times the country's total budget in 1938/9.

Political and Syndicate wives stationed in the monotonously boring terrain of the Gezira found two possible compensations. If so inclined, some could make lovely gardens, or indeed plant trees to enliven the landscape, because of the readily available irrigation; others could play more bridge and enjoy a more sophisticated social life then anywhere else in the country, outside Khartoum. And of course there were polo matches.

Elsewhere, up to Independence, polo was played on any flat, or comparatively flat, piece of land there happened to be; for instance in Khartoum the ground used lay in the desert beyond Omdurman. The expense of irrigating a green polo field was never even contemplated, so after the British had left, it was strange to read in a 1979 account that

The Sennar Dam in 1951

27

there were then no fewer than three polo fields within the race course at Khartoum, all of them irrigated and green.

A less fortunate legacy from the military days was that there were two British clubs in Khartoum – originally one for the officers and a second for other ranks. The distinction between the Sudan Club for senior officials and the Khartoum Club for junior officials persisted almost up to 1956. Membership of either club was determined by salary except in the case of the Political Service who, of course, and however poor, always belonged to the top club without question. Some members of other government departments resented this. They might not have minded so much had they known that, certainly before the war, a definite preoccupation with seniority existed within the Political Service itself. In 1927 a bride travelling on the train from Port Sudan found herself sharing a sleeper with another wife who, although they had travelled out by sea together, remained unknown to her. She was told in no uncertain terms, 'My husband is senior to yours, so you will have to have the top bunk.' Another bride making the same journey with her husband remembers, 'There were only two other passengers in the dining car. They were at the far end and were senior members of the Service. They took no notice of us at all – nor did we expect them to.'

This attitude was not entirely due to the inheritance of a military hierarchy. In England then, a respect for age and authority still obtained. Young men called their seniors (and often their fathers) 'Sir', and women addressed older women, even equals, as 'Mrs'. Christian names, even if known, were rarely used. (A young wife in the Sudan, told by her Governor to call him by his Christian name, could hardly bring herself to do so because, she thought, 'he must be at least forty'.) A social pecking order was observed by women, meticulously laid down by visiting-card etiquette. This being so, the bride who on arrival in Khartoum in 1927 was introduced by her husband to two senior wives should not have been surprised that she was 'greeted quite frostily'.

In Sudan before the war, even this strict observance of status went hand in hand with *noblesse oblige*. Many young wives remarked on, and remembered with gratitude, the hospitality of senior wives. 'Their kindness was universal. No one ever failed to help those who were young, bewildered, or in difficulties'. One young wife regretted that she could not repay all the hospitality, including a splendid feast on Christmas Day, that her Governor's wife had given her. 'Of course you can't,' she was told, 'just pass on the help to someone else'.

That young wife certainly did so, for she was later to become the Civil Secretary's wife in Khartoum, and her concern and readiness to help became a byword. Her generosity extended far beyond the normal regimental care and the traditional provision of last meal out, first meal in.

4 *Joining the Mess*

Wives realised on arriving in the country that they would not at first be able to understand Arabic, but it came as a shock to find that they could no longer understand their compatriots' language either. 'The few men in Malakal', recalls one wife, 'used so many Arabic words and local names that their conversation was incomprehensible to me and I felt completely excluded.' Arabic words did not merely pepper the conversation: they were an essential ingredient. Confusion became further confounded when every second Sudanese seemed to be called Muhammad or have Muhammad in his name.

'How could you be so stupid as not to realise that Muhammad Ahmad is a completely different person from Ahmad Muhammad? Why, one is the *Omda* and the other the *bash-katib*.'

'The who? The what?'

British nicknames could be no less misleading and, when completely unknown to the new wife, it was not always clear to whom they referred:

'I took a *shufti* (look) at old Tiger. He was champing at the bit. . .' (The wife envisaged a spirited Arab pony pawing the ground in his stable.) . . . 'so, without lighting his pipe, he shouted to the *marasla* to get his *sawaq* and went off with his *shunta*.' Ah! so Tiger had something to do with the railways? No. He had not. A *shunta* was a brief case, a *marasla* an office messenger and a *sawaq* a driver.

The use of Arabic was not the only cause of a wife's initial dismay. In 1926 a newly-arrived wife found herself to be the only woman in Geteina and remembers, 'through the long evenings the only topic of conversation was land registration and land resettlement on which my husband was working. Important as both may have been, they became

29

extremely monotonous. The six Province staff who were all bachelors were mostly very shy. Fortunately the majority played bridge, otherwise I really don't know what I would have done during those years.'

Such preoccupation with land resettlement in Geteina in 1926 resulted from the Government's decision to build a dam a little farther down the White Nile, at Jebel Aulia. Because of recurring difficulties with the Egyptian Government, ten years elapsed before this became an actuality. Riverain land resettlement remained an unending task for three main reasons: the annual Nile flood could sweep away what landmarks there were, submerge or alter existing islands, or change the shape of banks; secondly, inviolable laws of Muslim inheritance meant that a fifth cousin might have an irrefutable right to one sixty-fourth of a family plot; and finally, in a country where the extent of fertile land would always be strictly limited, arguments about boundaries could be acrimonious and bitterly contested.

Land registration was not only an important factor in establishing

A Bongo grave south east of Tonj

peace and security, it also protected the rights of the indigenous peoples. From the outset the Government had made it clear that foreigners were not to 'acquire' land and settle, as had been, and still was then, happening in neighbouring Kenya. This was a laudable, and for its time, a remarkably advanced precept. The resulting absence of settlers however does partly explain why lone S.P.S. wives felt more isolated than their Colonial Service equivalents.

In those early days a non-bridgeplaying wife could have found the supposedly social evenings very long indeed. The enthusiasm of the administrators would have ensured that they talked shop incessantly. There is nothing wrong with that; talking shop always has been, and ever will be, a useful and popular pastime. Unfortunately the new wife, who had perhaps been on her own all day, felt unable to participate and would have been piqued or disappointed at her exclusion. The men did not necessarily intend to disregard her but, used to an all-male society, they were slow to make concessions. This attitude was not peculiar. Sir Harold Macmillan, recalling his time at Oxford, wrote, 'Ours was an entirely masculine, almost monastic society. We knew of course that there were women's colleges with women students. But we were not conscious of either ... for practical purposes they did not exist.' Perhaps behind the overt criticism by these early wives lay a hidden dismay that neither did they seem to 'exist' either.

If they were ignored by the senior members of the Service for the reasons given by Macmillan, their neglect by the younger A.D.C.s could be attributed partly to shyness. These young administrators would have been to an all-male school, followed by a male college and would then have worked only with male compatriots. They might well have felt ill at ease with women as this anecdote bears out.

'I was due to arrive at Wadi Halfa in the Nile steamer early in the morning. Apparently my husband had found that he was able to arrive there only much later in the day so had therefore sent a message to the District Commissioner asking him to give me some help. I was asleep in my cabin at five in the morning when there was a knock on the door.

I threw on a dressing-gown and opened it. Outside stood the District Commissioner (not that I knew who he was) in uniform, with riding boots, and wearing a topi. He saluted – more than once – and invited me to breakfast three hours later. I felt like Queen Victoria, wakened by an invitation to breakfast rather than the throne. Except for the question of breakfast, he seemed inarticulate. He saluted yet again and went away. I got into bed again, terrified. Not only by the prospect of breakfast, but having no idea of where it would be and, even if I knew, how to get to it, and what to talk about when there. This last turned out to be the only real problem. By some means which I cannot clearly remember, but typical of the Sudan, all else was organised and the plan conveyed to me, even though I understood no Arabic. It transpired that I was pushed wildly along the little local railway line by an enthusiastic Sudanese porter in a sort of open chair-truck for one person. A camel would have been far less surprising. The Assistant District Commissioner joined us for a splendidly Edwardian five-course breakfast, and all three of us were seized up with a total inability to communicate.'

There was another occasion when the male and apparently silent service seemed unable to adjust to female company.

'I was travelling out to join my husband in Nyala, Western Darfur. He had been allowed to drive in to El Obeid to meet me, and managed to get to the station but almost immediately went down with malaria. (He had this every year for the first nine years of his service.) We were staying in the Deputy Governor's house, and as my husband had taken to his bed, I was left that evening to have dinner with seven unknown men. Kind as they were, and hard as I tried to be intelligent, I understood practically nothing of a conversation full of technicalities, references, obscure jokes and Arabic. After dinner, they all walked out into the garden. Thinking that perhaps we were going to sit on some kind of patio, I walked after them. They walked on into the desert, and only as far as that because they were pursued by me, and then began to fan out. Luckily the answer suddenly dawned on me – they were going to relieve themselves. This was a general Sudan custom. But no one beforehand had said to me, "Do you want the loo?" They just silently went.'

(In a different context, in a supposedly more civilised place, Khartoum, another wife was very annoyed with both the custom and the men who, she complained, had completely ruined her recently planted-out bed of petunia seedlings.)

Another male habit, firmly excluding wives, consisted of playing the old-boy network version of snap, and happened when two or three men were gathered together.

'Did you know Carruthers? He was in the second Division of the Umpteenth Foresters. Had a good war record.'

'No. He was a bit before my time. What about Blockson?'

'He was at Winnington too, wasn't he? He was in the desert, I believe, G.S.O.2 – under old Bumber. Remember him? Or was he senior to you?'

After half an hour of this exchange there would be an irresistible urge on the part of the totally excluded wife to call out 'Seventeen all – best of three.'

In 1934 one wife, recently down from Cambridge, found the conversation on social occasions 'boring and limited' for a different reason:

A Bongo stone

'When we were at Nyala, in Darfur, there were two other members of the Political Service, one of whom was married, making five of us altogether. We were sometimes joined by visitors from other government departments or from the Army. Whenever we met I was struck by the limits of the conversation; shooting, polo, horses, and lions – how many had been shot, when, where, and by whom. It was useless to start on books, pictures, even politics; the next minute we were sure to be back to lions.'

Before the war, away from university circles, it was considered a grave social disadvantage for a woman to be a blue-stocking. Men preferred wives to be decorative rather than clever, so nobody bothered about those who pined for intellectual stimulation.

Those men in Darfur added to their natural pleasure in recounting new experiences a determination never to admit, in public at least, any home thoughts from abroad. This resolve helped to foster what some interpreted as a restricted local interest and obliviousness to the outside world.

In fact members of the Sudan Political Service remained well aware of current world events because of a unique service. Every day each received a Reuter's telegram giving the main headlines. As a wife writing about 1926 recorded, 'the Reuter's telegram was a godsend. It resulted from a bargain made by Kitchener with the company, that they could send a reporter with the army up the Nile on condition that they continued to send a daily telegram after the war was over.' The caption 'army up the Nile' was still in use fifty years later.

Stunned as were some of the early, lone, wives by their reception in out-stations, most adapted to the prevailing customs and discourse within a matter of months. However, too early an attempt on their part to infiltrate the male preserve could have unexpected consequences:

'A judge on circuit was staying the night with us. By now I knew that a trek was rated, not by the scenery, but by the number of punctures and the number of creatures shot. Making conversation over drinks, I asked the judge whether he had shot any frangipani on the way up. I don't remember whether I was trying to say francolin (a gallinaceous bird like a partridge) or *gidad el wadi* (a guinea fowl). Anyway he burst into the loudest guffaw ever heard, because I had in fact asked him if he had shot an ornamental shrub with pretty scented flowers, especially planted outside rest houses. The still quiet evening was rent with bursts and shrieks of laughter. The servants rushed from the cookhouse at the back to see what all the excitement was about. The judge was an amusing talker and the story would certainly have been embellished as he travelled on round the province.'

During these timeless, limitless evenings, with no alternative entertainment to bridge, conversation was of great consequence. This society bred more than a handful of good raconteurs, who were popular and prized. One of these was a contract D.C., living in the trading post of Gambeila on the Abyssinian border.

'He was a well known character, tremendously worth meeting and quite unique. He was then sixty-two, had been in the army, a cowpuncher in Canada, a ship's purser and every other conceivable thing. Very large and most amiable, he now lived in this mile-square enclave in a frightful house with no glass in the windows and no veranda to keep out the heat. Without doubt one of the most amusing people I have ever met, and a brilliant raconteur, he told stories on and on and didn't really mind much if anyone were listening or not – he was so amused himself that the tears rolled down his cheeks. It seemed possible he could go on all night if no one stopped him.'

In Sudanese out-stations the arrival of a visiting official, whether a good raconteur or not, was an event to be anticipated with pleasure by the lone wife, just like the arrival of visitors in Jane Austen's day. When work necessitated a stay of more than one night, 'then', a wife remarked 'we soon reached a stage where we seemed to have known each other for years.' These officials usually came on their own, either being too young to have a wife or having had to leave their wife with their children; so wives in out-stations, especially before the war, invariably

A Zande witch doctor

lacked female companionship.

In compensation they soon began to learn more about the country as a whole and became increasingly interested in their husband's particular district. In 1928/9 a wife in Khashm el Girba, Kassala Province, 'drew diagrams of camel brands and camel saddlery for an article my husband was writing.' She also 'drew maps to show the position of new water holes that had just been dug.'

After the war one wife in Tonj, though no professional anthropologist, made a detailed study of the amazingly intricate Bongo grave poles. She had to use a local guide to find the graves, each individually hidden in the forest. She made detailed sketches of the elaborate funeral poles and wrote, 'they were wonderful examples of native craftsmanship, each one a composite of notched or carved wood, and different especially-made items of pottery. Each pole varied according to the prowess or past history of the departed.' She also tried to find out more about the magic Bongo stones as she had had a chance to witness their use. 'The Bongo stones were kept in an old pottery bowl in the Rain Chief's hut. They were thought by the tribe to have come down from Heaven, hence their power – and they could possibly have been meteorites.' Another interpretation was that they were ancient axe- and hammer-heads from long ago. 'Every Bongo really believed that if

35

he or she swore a lie on the stones he, and/or the relatives, would die, and their herd and house would be destroyed. When a native court over which my husband was presiding failed to determine which of three subjects had wounded a government policeman, they unanimously agreed to resort to the Bongo stones the next morning at dawn. Unfortunately two of the suspects were Jur who had less (or no) respect for the stones and they gave conflicting stories. In the end no verdict could be reached but the ceremony did at least clear the Bongo suspect.

Many wives looked back on these days of interested involvement with regret when, after their final return to the U.K., they found themselves perhaps the wife of a commuter and as such completely dissociated from their husband's work. In this new way of life, where it was easy enough to amass acquaintances, it took a long time to establish a lasting friendship.

*

5 Wives in the War

The majority of wives found the primary impact of the War to be their separation for long, or longer periods from their children or husbands. Although everyone had foreseen the possibility of war in 1939 since April, no-one was able to forecast the actual date of its declaration. So on 3 September it was pure chance whether members of the Sudan Political Service were on duty or on leave in the U.K. One wife recalls: 'I had been at home during the summer with our two children in Bexhill. My husband was due back in August for his leave. The shadow of war was over us and I began to wonder whether he would arrive in time. In fact we had had only a few days together when he was told to report to a ship in Glasgow within forty-eight hours. There was a rumour that all trains were to be requisitioned the next day for evacuating London school children so we set off that night in our old car. Luckily his mother's house was in Leicester, more or less on the way, so he was able to say "hello" and "goodbye" to all his relatives before taking the train to Glasgow. I drove back alone to Bexhill. The next day war was declared.

I had hoped to follow my husband with the children in due course but soon heard that the Sudan Government had put a ban on all passages for wives and children. Halfway through December I received a telegram from my husband to say that the ban had been lifted and I was to come out at once with our nanny and the children. Nanny, who had been growing increasingly nervous about the war and going to Africa, now definitely decided to go back to Ireland. In spite of this blow I was determined to join my husband so first thing next morning I went up to the Sudan Agent's Office in London. There were queues of us, all trying to book passages. Available shipping was very limited and almost the only option was a Lloyd Triestino boat sailing from one or other of the Italian ports. Unfortunately Italy was being very uncooperative over visas. Eventually all I was offered was a *third* class cabin on a boat leaving Genoa two days after Christmas provided, and only provided, that we each had a visa and a passport. At that point I hadn't even a nanny, let alone one with a passport. Undeterred I went round to Nursery World who were very helpful and a search produced not only a nanny willing to travel but one with a passport. I interviewed and engaged her the next morning. She turned out to be the best nanny I have ever known. She was interested in a foreign country, ready for anything and was always good-tempered.'

When the embargo on passages was lifted in December 1940 this wife was one of several who took the opportunity of returning to Sudan with the intention of staying there. But others, with children at school, decided to rejoin their husbands just for the Spring term. A few, not having to meet this deadline of the Easter holidays and lulled into a sense of normality by the six months of the phoney war, departed in March or April, planning to return to the U.K. later in the year. For them the breathtaking speed with which the invasion of the Netherlands was followed by the *débâcle* of Dunkirk on 27 May and then the fall of France on 17 June brought harrowing predicaments. 'By March 1940 we thought the phoney war might continue indefinitely. Our two children were settled in their prep schools and had two grandmothers and an aunt to look after them in the holidays so I decided to join my husband in Wad Medani. Just after I arrived the invasion of Denmark and Norway brought the phoney war to an abrupt end; had I known this was about to happen I doubt whether I would have left England.' Two years later she was to write to her mother, 'I wonder if you could have some photos taken of the children? Those you sent last summer are nearly worn out by being looked at and we are aching for some more.'

Another wife, who had stayed behind in England to have her first baby, travelled out in early May and was similarly caught. 'I decided to spend just six weeks with my husband but on my way out the Germans invaded the Low Countries, so I found myself stranded in the Sudan for four and a half years. This meant that I did not see my baby again until she was nearly five and my husband saw his second child (born in Khartoum in 1942) before he had ever seen his first.'

The unexpectedly fast collapse in Europe cost another family dear both financially and in nervous anxiety.

'When war was declared I stayed at home with my two small daughters. Early in 1940 my husband wrote to suggest I came out to join him for three months as after that he hoped to be released from the S.P.S. to go soldiering in the Middle East. So I left the little girls with their nanny staying with an uncle and aunt. I was booked on a plane to return to them in June but the week before I was due to leave, France fell and there I was stuck in the Sudan. How shattered I was when I thought of those little girls, only nine months and hardly two, in that elderly household, all too near the southern coast.

In the event my husband, like the majority of the Political Service, was not allowed to join up. We both felt desperate about our small daughters. Our nanny volunteered to bring the children out to us in South Africa. After several disappointments, when their berths were cancelled in favour of more important passengers, they eventually arrived in Durban. Here nanny, who had been splendid throughout, suddenly went to pieces and couldn't bear the sight of black faces. There was nothing for it but to find another job for her in England and send her home. At least we as a family were in the same continent for the rest of the war; but to achieve this we had had to sell our small cottage and all its precious contents.

I spent a pleasant year in Durban and then in November 1941 I started on the six-week journey to join my husband in Hasaheisa. As well as the children I had the twenty-one pieces of luggage which my mother had thought essential. They were a constant source of trouble and caused us to miss our train in Mombasa but we eventually reached Nairobi, then Namasagali and finally Juba where we boarded the Nile steamer.'

A week before France capitulated, Italy at last entered the War, on 10 June 1941. For the next year the Italian War in East Africa had a more immediate impact on those in Sudan than the continuing war in other zones. From the outset, Sudan's long border with Eritrea and Italian-occupied Ethiopia appeared vulnerable and became a source of anxiety. As Field-Marshall Wavell realised, 'all the Sudan Defence Force could do was to fight a delaying action against greatly superior forces.' The Sudan Government also realised that Kassala, which could not be held, lay no great distance from Khartoum. When Italy eventually did declare war there was not long to wait; in less than a month she took Kassala and two days later, on 6 July, Gallabat. This success might well have been followed up immediately, and the Sudan Government had every right to be apprehensive on this score even though one wife did not think so.

'When the Italians took Kassala there seemed no reason why they should not drive straight on to Khartoum and many people thought that they would. The army had no artillery or tanks and few aeroplanes. The R.A.F. set up a station near Erkowit and annoyed the Italians from there. I don't think they did much damage but they certainly made our one 'hill station' untenable for civilians as the Italians

Three Beja tribesmen of the Red Sea Hills

naturally retaliated. After several hours crouched in the khor, while they bombed the main building, we decided to return to Khartoum North with the children. Our house was in the railway compound and my husband obtained some very fine girders to build an excellent air-raid shelter, but after a few alarms a scorpion was found in the shelter and my English nanny refused to take the children into it again. The Secretariat then became slightly hysterical and sent out two circulars urging officials to send their children out of the Sudan. The second contained a questionnaire asking how many rooms we had and how many soldiers we could accommodate and it also pointed out that civilians would not be entitled to medical attention in the event of occupation. As my husband had a full-time job running his district he thought it better to make arrangements for us to leave while we could. Kenya was then suffering a famine and refused to take any more refugees. Somebody suggested Southern Rhodesia, so we went down to the Chamber of Commerce for information. We found an advertisement for accommodation on farms for three months at 8/- (40p) a head a day. The only trouble was that the advertisement was several years old. However we wrote a letter to the Secretary of the Settlers Society in Umtali which was the first place on the Beira–Salisbury railway. (We would be flying to Beira.) Suddenly we were offered a passage on a flying-boat. We were allowed to take only twenty kilos of luggage each, but none for Judy as she was under three. As there had been no time for an answer from Umtali it was a little apprehensively that I set out.

We eventually got off the train at Umtali in the dark. The 'white' hotel, a long way up the steep hill, was full because of a conference, so we were advised to try the Railway Hotel. This was decidedly second class and the bar was already full and noisy. There was no lounge. Upstairs our bedroom could have come straight out of a Wild West film; it was ventilated by opening the top half of the door, like a stable. The hotel keeper was very kind to us and sent some trays up to our rooms. Gradually the noise below died down. The next morning we woke to bright sunshine and saw the peaceful little town all wreathed in jacaranda trees in full bloom. I was then told that the Settlers Society had been disbanded but that the secretary still lived in Umtali and in fact ran the local newspaper. I would find him in his office even though it was Sunday. So I toiled up the hill and found this little man, hard at work, wearing a green eye shade. I began my story. He said he was there to meet me. This quite bowled me over, but he explained that our letter had been delivered to him and that he had arranged for a farmer on the Vumba (about twenty-two miles from Umtali and several thousand feet higher) to fetch us in her lorry that afternoon. So for the next three months we lived up a

41

mountain with the most hospitable woman I have ever met. They had made a swimming pool and dammed the little river for crop water, at the same time stocking it with black bass, so I was able to have great fun with a fishing rod. Unfortunately nanny did not have quite such a good time, so after her holiday in Salisbury she was most anxious for us to move there. I could not really afford this as I knew it would cost me more than the twenty-four shillings a day on the farm but I did find a clean, reasonably cheap boarding house. I managed to land a job in the Statistical Department on the strength of my maths degree and I also found a school for Hugo. This only lasted a few weeks as he brought home the prevailing whooping-cough. We then had a dismal time as first Judy, then nanny and then even I contracted the disease.'

While this wife was in Rhodesia those remaining in Sudan, especially if in a province on the Italian frontier, found themselves under threat of further attack. Some wives had husbands serving in Wad Medani, the headquarters of the Blue Nile Province during the summer of 1940. One commented, 'when the Italian forces were massing on the border it seemed only a matter of time before the province would be over-run. The men were all given temporary commissions in the Sudan Defence Force to ensure their military status should they be captured. They kept the necessary badges in their pockets ready to be fastened on to their shoulder tabs. Air raid shelters were dug and the police trained as aircraft spotters. Fortunately the summer rains meant that an overland attack using motor transport was less likely'.

One of the wives became a cipher clerk.'As there was petrol rationing I rode a donkey which had only one pace, a fast amble, and which was oblivious of all traffic, and simply tied him up outside the office. The decoding was mostly very boring work indeed; and it often seemed to me unnecessary as well because every absurd detail was sent in code. For instance one telegram read, 'Sergeant Blank has left his hat on the Kosti boat', another that a large consignment of loo paper was imminent; and on Christmas Eve an urgent one transpired to be from a senior officer enquiring about the sand-grouse shooting. Still, made into jokes, these gave light relief. By September we had become less tense and not a little cheered by the inexplicable inactivity of the Italian Air Force. The code name for the Italian war was Gadwell, appropriately enough a dull kind of duck and a slow flyer.'

Another wife replaced a confidential clerk in the province headquarters. 'My arrival in this exclusively male set-up so embarrassed one member that he always averted his eyes whenever we met in the passage or on the stairs.'

These and other wives were also busy away from the offices. 'There were always people passing through. I can remember a desperate feel-

Jebel at Kassala

ing sometimes that our home was nothing but a canteen. Often by bed-time I could have cried with tiredness. Luckily I always recovered the next day. By November reinforcements were arriving and prepara-tions were in progress for an advance into Ethiopia. By January the place teemed with British troops: I think about 15,000 passed through altogether. We always tried to give them a cup of tea at the station. We boiled water in four-foot high oil drums and at the warning bell put in a pound of tea and let it go on boiling away. The resulting liquid was black with a thick dusty froth. Curiously all the troops preferred this brew to ice-cold fresh lemon even though the shade temperature was 112°F.'

It was not until February 1941 that the famous siege of Keren began. Later described as one of the hardest battles ever fought, the siege lasted for fifty-three nerve-racking days. Victory was not conceded until 26 March. Total surrender and the end of the Italian Empire in East Africa followed on 16 May, much to the relief of all those in Sudan.

From now on wives and families could use with more safety the gov-ernment 'hill station' of Erkowit. It may have been 3,000 ft. up in the Red Sea Hills, but any similarity to an Indian hill station ended there. Characteristically of any building or amenity in the Sudan, Erkowit was spartan compared to its equivalent in India, merely resembling a glorified rest-house – not surprisingly, as that is exactly how it began. It had been chosen as a rest camp by General Sir Reginald Wingate, Governor-General of the Sudan from 1899 to 1916. A nearby view-point, from which could be seen Suakin and the sea, was still called

43

'Kitty's Leap' after his wife. (Research reveals that she did not leap from the point; merely walked to it!) The Governor of Kassala also had a hot-weather house here and at the start of the '39 war the Sudan Railways, who were to run the complex on *en pension* terms, put up more buildings. 'There was a central two-storeyed building,' writes a wife, 'surrounded by individual units. Each of these had two bedrooms with a bath and loo and were ideal for families. Tennis on the two courts could be of a remarkably high standard, partly because there was an R.A.F. station nearby. Apart from that there was nothing to do and a great deal of bridge had to be played. The surrounding country consisted of rock and sand dotted with euphorbia trees but it was greener than elsewhere in the Red Sea Hills because of the *shabura* (mist). (On a long walk I once became lost in this and had difficulty in regaining the "hotel".)'

Wives not allowed to remain in their husband's districts during the rains would come to Erkowit until they could go on leave together. Families finding the heat of the summer months oppressive also came here for a break. Some wives who could afford it preferred to go straight to Kenya and wait there for their husbands. Their favourite resort, the Brackenhurst Hotel at Limuru, became almost a Sudan club. One veranda's length of half-a-dozen single rooms was habitually occupied during the war by temporarily-widowed Sudan wives and their children. Much as the height and the marvellous Garden-of-Eden scenery was savoured by these 'Sudanis', they were discomfited by the

Foreshore at Wad Medani

44

all too evident truculent and hostile attitude of some of the Kikuyu, so noticeable after the universally friendly reaction of the locals in Sudan. (Mau Mau troubles did not break out until 1953.)

Not all leaves were spent 'south of the border'. Even before the war and before home leave was stopped, some members of the Political Service chose to go to Cyprus or the Middle East instead of to the U.K. One wife recalls,

'We had three leaves in what was then called Palestine, after the last of which our son was born in Alexandria in 1944. My journey back from there was fraught with difficulties. First we had to wait in Cairo until the level of the Nile was right for the paddle steamer to travel to Wadi Halfa. When I arrived at Shellal I found our bookings had been muddled up and I had to wait for another boat on which there were no Europeans to help. At Wadi Halfa the train on which we had been booked had left. We boarded another which constantly stopped so that the line, damaged by the rains, could be inspected. We eventually arrived in Khartoum thirty-six hours late. There, met by my husband, we all piled into a car. That might have been the end of our troubles but the car stuck fast in the mud almost within sight of our house in Hasaheisa. We had to send for the *syce* to bring two donkeys for the children. My husband and I sloshed through the mud carrying the Moses basket with our three-month-old son between us. I began to feel I had had enough of the Sudan.'

When not on leave, wives in Khartoum and other centres cheerfully and willingly turned their hands to all the jobs usually allocated to women in wartime, to the many chores normally under the aegis of the Red Cross, of which there was a flourishing branch in Khartoum, and to the then Women's Voluntary Service, now W.R.V.S. In particular they helped to entertain the troops. It was at this time that the Clergy House suppers after the Sunday evening service started, primarily for the benefit of the Forces, but they continued to be a popular social occasion for many years to come.

The Second World War affected Political Service wives in three principal ways. First, it proved them to be not as fragile as had been supposed and that they could survive, and indeed had survived, the hottest months of the year. Consequently, from now on they tended to come out to the country for longer periods. Secondly, it was found that British babies could be born in Khartoum Hospital without disadvantage or mishap. Thirdly, not only had the war accelerated social change, but concurrently and more pertinently, the old guard had reached the end of their service and with them had departed much of the previous pomp and circumstance. For instance, governors no longer donned full-dress uniform with plumes in their helmet. Socially, the Sudan Political Service had become much more relaxed.

45

6 *First time out – Post-War*

After the War, a firm using Vikings was chartered to ferry personnel to and fro. They operated from Blackbushe near Camberley, Surrey. The first night was spent in Malta and only by the evening of the second day was Wadi Halfa thankfully reached. Subsequently more powerful planes were used which did not have to refuel so frequently. They now departed from, and arrrived at, Khartoum Airport, thus saving the delay and nuisance of a train journey from Wadi Halfa. There was a second bonus: now that the journey out and back took only two days instead of four, everyone had the advantage of two whole precious extra days in the U.K. This was because officially each person's allocated leave was reckoned from the moment of crossing the Sudan border.

In the late Autumn of 1949 one of these larger planes crashed into the sea near Sicily. In spite of lifebelts several children were among the casualties because they were swept away by the waves and irretrievably lost in the dark. Following this tragedy a husband wrote home and told his wife to make sure to bring a length of rope with her when she travelled out so that she could link the children together.

'I had stayed behind after our leave for the birth of our third child. Anxious as I was to get back to the Sudan I anticipated the journey on my own, with children under five, with some trepidation. It was obvious that two hands would be inadequate; even six could hardly have managed two small children, a carrycot and all the innumerable bags and packages needed on the plane, not to mention passports, handbags and landing cards. Besides all this, my husband had told me to take some rope. At Blackbushe we had just been moved from one waiting area to the embarkation lounge. Suddenly an air hostess swept through the door, holding up a coil of rope, and calling in a loud voice, "Does this belong to anybody?" Rather sheepishly I said it was mine. "What on earth do you need that for?" another passenger asked. (So far, we had all very carefully avoided mentioning the plane crash three weeks before. Looking back on it now this seems quite extraordinary. I suppose then we were all so used to underplaying anything unpleasant.) I wasn't quick enough to think up a phoney reason, so I just explained why I had the rope. Cleverly this man turned it into a joke and started interviewing all the unaccompanied men as if for a job, turning them down if they couldn't produce evidence of sufficient swimming prowess. By the time we boarded the plane he had detailed three of the best swimmers to look after each of the three children. "Now", he said "you can leave the rope behind". As an afterthought he added "I suppose *you* can swim?" I had to confess that I loathed the sea and could hardly keep my chin above the waves. "Well, you'd better take the rope after all – and I'll hang on to the other end."

None of these precautions was necessary because that flight and every other for the next six years was accomplished without mishap. Much to their relief, wives now tended to travel to and fro with their husbands. Only when school terms necessitated an earlier return did they once more have to travel on their own.

A Nile steamer postboat

The foreshore at Malakal

Post-war wives enjoyed another advantage. Before coming out for the first time they were able to get advice from seasoned campaigners about what clothes and essentials to bring with them. Even so, such vitally important items as books were not always mentioned. One wife's account can speak for itself.

'I met P. on his leave in 1947 when I was working in London and we agreed to get married on his next leave home the following year. I knew a bit about the Sudan and what to expect in the way of heat and flies as I had been stationed in Alexandria for two years when I was in the W.R.N.S. during the war.

In July 1948 we travelled out by air with overnight stops, eventually arriving at Wadi Halfa. From there we took the train to Khartoum, and then another on to Kosti. This last lap of some two hundred and fifty miles was an overnight journey. At Kosti we moved onto the Post boat. This was an ancient-looking stern-wheeler paddle-steamer, with six or more freight barges lashed ahead and alongside. It had a wood-burning engine. The front deck of the boat was roofed over and enclosed in mosquito wire so here we were able to sit in cool comfort during the ten days it took to reach Malakal, headquarters of Upper Nile Province.

Malakal was not so much a town, as a handful of run-down bungalows. I think the main street may have been paved but the others were just mud. Of course it looked its worst in the rains and I can remember thinking it a dreary and ghastly shanty town. One house, pointed out to me as my father-in-law's when he had been Governor here some fifteen years earlier, amazed me by its shabbiness. The two main shops belonged to Greeks: Stavros and Limnios. They sold almost everything from food to nails, ropes to lamps, most items being covered in a thick layer of dust because they had been there so long. One pleasant surprise was to find dress-making material which was still rationed in austerity England.

Before I left, my mother-in-law had insisted that I should have a felt hat. When she had been out with my husband, then a small boy, she had so instilled into him the importance of always wearing a hat that he had thought then that, were it to come off, he would drop dead! In fact by this time we all wore dark glasses and rarely a hat.

Unfortunately, as we arrived at the end of July in the rainy season, all the women with the exception of one nursing sister were on leave. As I had never been able to stand heat easily and found high humidity oppressive, I began to wonder how I could possibly endure it all.

After a night or two in Malakal we travelled further south in the smaller Province steamer to the District headquarters in Fangak.

A Nuer village during the dry weather

49

Nuer in dugout canoe taking cattle across river

This was approximately one hundred and fifty miles south of Malakal up a branch of the Nile known as the Zeraf river. It was a not unattractive place. From our house, near the river, we could see the crocodiles and hear the hippos. I often used to walk in a government garden nearby, planted with citrus trees. Our mud-brick house had a thatched roof, as did the office and all the Sudanese officials' houses. I couldn't speak to the servants as I knew neither Nuer nor Arabic. Philip always had to act as interpreter, but as he went off to the office after breakfast and didn't get back until past two, I found it very lonely indeed. Never before or since have I longed so much for a female companion. I had only a few books and no music as our cases had not yet arrived. Time passed very slowly.

In the afternoons we sometimes went riding. I had not ridden much before coming to the Sudan but the Arab ponies were small and I usually managed all right. Once though, just as we turned to go back, the horse made a sudden headlong dash for his stable. I lost my stirrups and then the reins but, clinging on to his neck, somehow managed not to fall off. It was very frightening as the horse was making straight for the river and, not believing he would ever stop, I saw myself plunging into the crocodile-infested Zeraf.'

It usually took 'new girls' a year to become acclimatised to the country. At first they invariably suffered from either frequent bouts of dysentery or, as this wife goes on to say, from a recurring septic throat.

'During my first tour I constantly had a sore throat. Once when it was very bad we were in Malakal and the Sudanese doctor cured me with penicillin. In our station there was only a medical dresser and an assistant. Before I came out my husband found he had a very bad rash on his face. The dresser said he had a shaving rash and the assistant thought it was syphilis! Fortunately the Province vet was passing through, recognised the rash as impetigo (caught from handling tribute money), and cured it with gentian blue or some other drug he kept for animals.

This vet was called Thompson, and as there was also an agriculturist and a D.C. in the Province with the same name, they were generally referred to as Thompson the cowman, Thompson the ploughman and Thompson the Member for Bum, Bum being a small village near Kodok, the D.C.'s station.

As the Nuer were a cattle-owning tribe, flies annoyed us perpetually. In spite of this we kept surprisingly well and neither of us succumbed to dysentery or tummy trouble. All the men told me I ought to drink whisky every evening, as a prophylactic. I really loathed the stuff, but it was only later when I went to Malakal after the wives had returned that I learned whisky was not essential. From then on, with great relief, I drank lime instead. Of course we took Paludrin against malaria and I wore mosquito boots in the evenings as a precaution.

Out of doors we used to sit in a mosquito-proof room or tent because there were always so many flies, stink bugs and innumerable other insects. When it was dark, even more were attracted by the Petromax lamp which we consequently had to keep outside the net. The light inside was hardly good enough for sewing. When my husband was not studying for his Nuer exam we used to play card games, piquet or bezique. Later on he taught me how to play bridge, providentially, for soon afterwards we travelled on a steamer where there happened to be just three, consequently very frustrated, bridge players. More by luck than judgement I managed not to disgrace myself on that occasion and have played bridge ever since.

The Nuer were friendly and cheerful. The young girls with their lovely figures and long slender legs, were very attractive to look at. After marriage and one or two children, they unfortunately deteriorated. When the children were weaned after two years' breast feeding there was always a distressingly high mortality rate, usually due to dysentery. On the whole they seemed a naturally happy and contented people. Perhaps they had the answer to life: few possessions, simple food and very little work!

I always enjoyed trekking whether on foot or in the lorry. But looking back now I wish I had had some medical training before I went out; we used to see so many ailing children and some with eyes blocked up with pus. I also wish I had felt better and had had more

A group of Nuer girls

energy. In spite of having been five years in the W.R.N.S., and being twenty-six when I married, I was still very ignorant and unsophisticated. Modern girls now are so much more sensible and independent, and from a much earlier age too. On the whole, though, I wouldn't have missed any of my time in the Upper Nile.'

Several years after Independence, when this wife and others had long since left, a woman journalist from Europe wrote with great braggadocio of standing where no white woman had stood before, surrounded by menacing natives holding spears. She was admired and believed by all but a few Political Service wives, who were undoubtedly quietly amused.

By the end of the nineteen-thirties social attitudes had already begun to change in England and the rate of change had been accelerated by World War II. Various conventions such as calling, with its attendant etiquette, became less important, and Christian names more frequently and more quickly used. These and other changes percolated slowly through to Sudan so that now friendships cut more easily across rank and different government departments. With transfers occurring every two or three years, new teams and new friendships constantly formed, helping to 'create a camaraderie seldom found elsewhere in the modern world.'

7 A Rather Superior Tent

Since 1899, for about twenty-six years, only bachelors had lived in out-stations. They retained a stiff if sweaty upper lip, disdaining comfort and living as if on active service. To their austere quarters came the first wives, two years after the Egyptian Army mutiny in 1924. Looking back on their first house a wife admits: 'I am surprised that I accepted some of the discomforts without realising that they could be alleviated quite easily. I just thought it was the way of life in the Sudan and decided to enjoy it all.' A resigned acceptance was shown by another wife: 'Living conditions outside Khartoum appeared more tough and basic than I could ever have imagined. I was not sure as regards housing whether the British simply lacked experience, or imagination, or money; but since they had settled for this kind of life, I could only assume that it was rather splendid of them and it would be most un-British of me to complain.'

One reason why the houses were initially so basic was that the men rarely entered them. They may have taken lunch and a siesta indoors but they sat and dined outside, then slept under the stars. For roughly half of the month they went on trek, so they regarded the house understandably as a rather superior tent. When wives came out and conditions could have been improved, they found little personal inclination to alter anything, and officially there was no money. The country remained poor. In 1900, with gum arabic virtually the only export, the total annual revenue did not exceed £126,000. When various agricultural projects had slowly increased the revenue to nearly £7 million, the world-wide recession of 1931 had a disastrous effect on the economy and this figure was not attained again until 1945, by which time stringent economy had become a habit, if not a way of life.

The majority of houses in out-stations were elongated versions of the local *tukl,* usually partitioned into three-by-five-foot high mud walls. There was nothing wrong with mud and thatch in theory, both being good insulators. Sometimes though the thatch let in rain. 'The rain was soon torrential and came through the roof in several places. We had pails and bowls everywhere trying to catch the streams of water coming down.' A judgement came from another wife, also referring to the 1920s. 'We had a charming mud brick house in Talodi but there was no glass in the windows. I don't know why, as the Greeks had glass in their houses and shops. When there was a storm I had to stand in the middle of the room to escape the rain lashing in through the mosquito wire.' The absence of glass was noted in another province: 'The windows had mosquito netting in them but the doors had none, so in due course we both got malaria, fortunately not at the same time.'

A wife who came out as a bride in the nineteen-thirties recalls her first home in the Sudan:

'B. had sensibly refrained from describing our house in any detail. No bath, except for a small green concrete square into which hot water could be poured; windows of wire meshing, with shutters to keep out the wind, if not the sand; and room walls not actually attached to the ceiling. Unaware of such gaps I had brought out some attractive curtains. The moment I put them up, rats ran delightedly down them from the roof.

Once, while waiting for my husband to appear for lunch at two-thirty, I glanced across at our water jug. A very large rat was standing on its hind legs, freely lapping. On B's return I said, "I'm afraid I can't stay married to anyone who has rats drinking his drinking water. I am leaving you." B. replied, "How actually will you leave?" Lacking a camel or any other practical transport to the railhead five hundred miles away, that put a stop to the conversation.'

In the province headquarters, houses for the more junior members of the government were rectangular sheds made of concrete bricks. Instead of thatch, they had corrugated tin roofs, absolutely splendid for attracting the heat of the mid-day sun. A wife wrote prosaically, 'In Khartoum and the larger towns there were some two-storeyed houses but the standard Sudan Government house was a bungalow. Planned by men for men, the lay-out was standard too, serviceable but hardly imaginative, only the number of rooms varying according to the seniority of the occupants. Our 'B' type bungalow in Wad Medani was typical — the rooms were arranged 'in line ahead' starting with the sitting room and dining room divided by an archway and continuing through two connecting bedrooms to the bathroom beyond. All the main rooms had french windows and electric fans. A wide veranda ran round three sides of the house, and part of this was enclosed in mosquito wire. Dur-

Making mud bricks in Darfur

ing the rains it provided a good place to sleep and at other times of the
year it could in the cooler hours be used as an extra sitting room.'

In that hot and sweaty climate the bathroom could be considered
almost the most important room in the house. Contrary to any wife's
expectation it turned out to be the smallest, the stuffiest and the most
primitive room − bar one − of them all. Baths were rarely of the
enamel type. As late as 1945 a new house in Waat was built with the
usual cemented sunken square in the corner. Sometimes civilisation
reached the height of a plug and an outlet but more often than not servants would have to scoop out the water with the ubiquitous four-gallon
petrol tin.

Taps were fitted to basins, the cold one being fed by gravity feed
from a small tank outside. If the hot tap worked in a bath this was considered four-star sophistication. Hot water could be piped from a ten-
gallon drum, heated by a wood fire, some distance from the thatch and
the house. Equally frequently, hot water was carried in by the servants,
again using the four-gallon petrol tin. It was often possible to achieve a
depth of two inches, particularly in the cement square type of bath.

In out-stations prisoners supplied the water to domestic premises.
They would fill a water tank on wheels which creaked along at a snail's

55

pace, drawn by a plodding ox. Alternatively donkeys could be used. 'A *tulba* (gang) of prisoners drove the donkeys, across whose backs two goatskins of water were slung. There was always a policeman in charge who carried a gun (I doubt if it was ever loaded). In order to avoid bilharzia the washing water was humped up to a tank on the roof where it had to stand for twenty-four hours before being used.' Bilharzia was not the only hazard on trek when having a bath. 'Once in a rest house, I was just about to step into a round canvas bath when I saw a large spider between it and me. At that precise moment the hurricane lamp went out. I couldn't call for help as D. was sitting just outside the doorless opening, talking to village elders. I just had to leap over the intervening space, hoping I would miss the spider. A few seconds later something swooshed through my hair. It was a bat. It continued to whirl round my head while I sat in the bath, nerving myself to renegotiate the spider. The men continued to chatter on outside.'

So much for the bath. What about the other plumbing? There was none. The loo was a wooden seat or box over a heavy bucket of gigantic proportions. Whether in the house itself or some yards down the 'garden', there was always the risk that the user could be enthroned just when the iron flap at the back was lifted up and the bucket heaved away. In out-stations the (unfortunate) man plodded silently into the compound on bare feet. He was not always so unobtrusive. A governor's wife in Darfur remembers 'sitting with dinner guests in the garden and receiving a smart salute from the bucket men as they trotted past with the buckets on their heads.' An even more surprising interruption occurred in another province, also just after the War. 'Once when we were out to dinner and in the middle of our meal a bucket man marched straight through the dining room. I have never forgotten my utter amazement. Apparently there was no other way to the loo.'

In Khartoum and the larger towns the night-soil men operated a long camel-drawn cart on shrieking iron-rimmed wheels.Visiting foreigners, right up to 1955, often wondered why this malodorous mediaeval system still obtained in this so called capital 'city'. There was a short answer: no money. Only one residence in Khartoum boasted a water-closet and that was the Palace. For some reason there happened to be also one house in Atbara that had managed to achieve this distinction.

'When we went to Atbara in 1949 we had the priceless advantage of living in the only house in the town which had a water closet. The only snag was that frogs bred in the cess-pit below. It was not unusual to be greeted on an early morning visit by three or four pairs of froggy eyes goggling up from the bowl. This had an unfortunate effect on our daughter Julia who has had a frog phobia ever since.'

In those days the best possible option was Bromo, a kind of tissue paper. A wife wrote, 'I can vividly remember our sufragi who like every other Muslim used water for the same purpose, saying to me soon after I had arrived, "*Al-waraqa* (the paper) *ma binfa* (does not work)." To which, even had my Arabic been up to it, there was no reply.' The present day soft paper-hanky version had not then been invented, or had not reached the out-stations.

Apart from that necessity even drinking water was not readily available away from the main towns, and always had to be filtered and then boiled. Water was then kept in a *zir*, a large earthenware Ali Baba jar reminiscent of a Cretan amphora without the handles, which stood in a specially-made shelter of openwork bricks, dripping into a covered bucket underneath. Moisture evaporating from the outside of the earthenware pot cooled the water within. That was the theory. Water could be further cooled by the precursor to the paraffin refrigerator, an 'Icy-ball'. This was a Swiss contraption and consisted of two metal retorts looking like a dumb-bell. One sphere was enclosed in a cupboard along with the water and other items to be cooled. The other bowl contained a chemical heated by a lamp underneath. It worked on the same principle as the refrigerator but the system had to be renewed every day. The operation of this Heath Robinson affair was not as simple as it sounds: 'On one memorable occasion the Icy-ball overheated and began to hiss in a sinister manner. The *sufragi* rushed it out on to the lawn where, after forming a gigantic ball of ice, it finally exploded.'

Paraffin refrigerators began to be used before the war. A wife coming out for the first time in 1938 remarked on a much prized secondhand one, 'newly acquired to celebrate my arrival.' These refrigerators were not trouble-free either. The wick of the lamp needed constant maintenance, and a strong wind or *habub* could blow it out, often just when the ice was most needed. Every time the door was opened any cool air quickly escaped and was replaced by the oven-hot equivalent before the door could be shut again. For this reason, the Scottish wife of a vet renowned for her culinary prowess would solemnly sit in front of her refrigerator all morning to prevent her cook from continually opening and shutting the door, if she wanted to ensure that her soufflé for the evening dinner party set properly. Ice was a luxury and a continuous supply for a number of guests a triumph of no mean order.

Once paraffin refrigerators were available, wives stored the filtered and boiled water in them in empty gin bottles. Needless to say, mistakes were frequent. One couple gave gin to a missionary instead of water and soon afterwards the husband found he was using gin for his watercolour painting. These were not the only misfortunes to occur,

'When I travelled with the children I used to take a case of old gin bottles filled with water. One evening I started as usual to reconstitute powdered milk. I beat and beat but it was unduly obstinate and

I handed it over to my husband. He did no better. Eventually he gave a suspicious sniff; I had picked up the wrong bottle and stupidly finished off the remains of the month's gin ration. It was just as well that gin and powdered milk did *not* mix.'

After the war some Sudanese workers in the Gezira cotton scheme, earning good money, were able to buy refrigerators too. There was a joke going round that one new owner could not think what to put in his refrigerator so he put his clean clothes in on the shelves. This was not as stupid as it sounds. Some time before this a Political Service wife regretted that she did not have a second refrigerator because she would 'so like to put her sheets in it in order to have a really cool bed to sleep in.' To own two refrigerators would have been an unheard-of (and unpardonable) luxury. To own just a modern trouble-free electric one was as unimaginable as suddenly waking up in Greenland's icy mountains.

Electricity itself was a novelty, the majority of wives spending more years without it than with it. No one in an out-station expected to enjoy the benefit of an electric ceiling fan. 'In our Talodi house (which in earlier times had been a governor's) there was a *punkah*. I felt that I just couldn't ask a servant to sit outside and pull it for me all morning; it was

Dinka thatching a roof of a hut

58

too like slave labour.' In an attempt to keep out some of the heat, servants would come round immediately after breakfast to shut up the house, closing all windows and shutters if, that is, there were any to shut. The wife would then sit in a darkened room which gradually became hotter and hotter as the morning wore on. Small wonder that a wife was delighted to find, on her return from having a baby in Kenya, that her husband had been transferred to Medani, a province headquarters. 'It was really nice to be back in a place with electricity and to be able to have not only fans but electric light instead of very hot Tilley lamps. I had enjoyed Singa and was sad not to see it again but it was no place for a baby.'

Wad Medani would also have been an easier place in which to have a child's cot or playpen made. Carpenters were good at copying illustrations but as they had no cause to use some of the items themselves there were often some functional mistakes, as one wife ruefully recalls.

'When I was having our first baby in Khartoum the Governor-General's wife (because I happened to be staying in the Palace) kindly organised the making of a cot for me at the Stores and Ordnance department in record time. She showed them a picture from an Army and Navy Stores catalogue. It was a superb cot. In fact, as I was to discover later, the most superior in the country. She had had it made extra long so that our child would not outgrow it too quickly. It was so well made, and so large and so heavy that we could not take it on trek with us and had to have another cheap one made locally. This one was racketed to bits in a few years; the other I'm sure would have survived at least twenty-four children. This was never proved, as we had only three.'

Most adults slept on a local *anqarayb* which could be made anywhere from light local unpolished wood. The woven rope base was both practical and comfortable. The cotton-filled mattress was equally cheap. Apart from this one item of furniture many young administrators, who tended to be on trek far more than their seniors, simply made do with their trek equipment while they were still bachelors.

'When I first arrived in 1948 we had nothing to sit on but our trek furniture. It was a great day when our cases at last arrived from England and we were able to unpack our wedding presents and various other belongings including a very nice picnic basket. In fact this, and many other things soon became dilapidated wrecks. The servants achieved this premature deterioration through enthusiasm rather than any destructive spirit. Having no possessions themselves they had no idea how to look after them. Not surprisingly they could not distinguish between shiny metal that had to be scrubbed and silver that ought to be gently polished. In the south they cleaned everything with literal vim and vigour.

We then had some furniture made out of local mahogany. The settees and chairs were comfortable but very heavy and difficult for the servants to move in and out of the house every day. I also asked for a kidney-shaped dressing table. When it arrived it was found to be so enormous that it was ever afterwards known as the 'D.C.'s desk'. Everyone had an easily-made wooden garden-seat type of sofa with two matching chairs, so wives showed their taste, or lack of it, in the material used to cover the rectangular cushions. Some, to their chagrin, inherited covers chosen by their *sufragi* during their husband's bachelor days. As so often with the Government, the expense of effecting an improvement could not be justified. In any case, after the War the choice of material in the local *suq* remained so limited that in Khartoum a dressmaking wife might any day have found herself sitting on the self-same material.

Anyone bringing out good furniture from the U.K. was pitied rather than envied by those who knew only too well what would happen to it in a few years. It was not just the destructive moves; the extreme dryness cracked the wood and made the veneer peel. In the south humidity did not help either: 'All the drawers of our softwood furniture swelled in the rains and had to be planed down. Consequently in the dry season there were large gaps.' This was one reason why old stagers made do with glorified packing cases, disguised with a bit of material. It was a reason why a wife had cause to complain, 'I cannot think why two generations of men had not managed to get carpenters to make cupboard doors and drawers a rational shape.' It was not only men who failed to succeed, as this article written retrospectively in 1944, and reproduced by permission of *Punch*, bears out.

The carpenter was always changing his clothes. He wore a shirt and shorts with Western bonhomie for a bit: then he would suddenly reappear with an aura of profound holiness, in a snow-white robe and turban, making it impossible to haggle over the prices. Dressed one way or the other, his passion remained a cosy chat rather than his craft. He came to see me carrying an immense pile of back-number catalogues from Haple.

"Choose what you will!" he exclaimed, throwing open the page at a bedroom suite in pickled walnut, "and I shall construct it. When it is finished, you dislike it, you would it had been otherwise – very well then, speak!"

I said that, anyhow, we did not want an immense double divan bed from Haple's with a pink shaded lamp attached. He seemed amazed. I said that we wanted some dining-room chairs, a tea-table, and that he should paint some of our furniture yellow. He adapted himself agreeably.

"Many and various," he said, with interest, "are the dining-room chairs I have made. Once I made chairs for the house of one Sir Ball Biscuit, whom you may know . . ."

I thought I did not; but after a moment there sprang to mind a distinguished administrator of the 'thirties called Sir Paul Pesketh.

"Now the chairs of Sir Ball Biscuit," said the carpenter, "may well last over a hundred years. If they do, none will be less surprised than I. The wood was good wood; hard, endurable, of our own country, beautiful . . ."

"It might do for us," I said.

He bent his brows on this egotistical preoccupation with one's own affairs.

"How do I tell," he asked, "whether you wish your chairs bolished or no bolish?"

"You cannot tell," I agreed, "until we have told you. And we cannot tell you until we have chosen the wood."

He glanced suddenly at his watch .

"Let us speak further of it tomorrow," he cried, and wheeled his bicycle into place.

"The bolish upon the chairs of Sir Ball Biscuit," he went on, composing himself to mount, "was such that guests recognised in it their own faces. The arms of the chairs were carved with much fantasia. They went round and round and round as it might be the coils of a deadly snake."

"Be that as it may." I replied.

He whizzed away, pedalling furiously.

"Your excellency spoke of a tea-table," he said, arriving at tropical noon the following day. "Many and various are the tea-tables I have . . ."

"Let us not speak of them, I said. "What *we* want . . ."

"Choose," he said generously, and cast Haple's catalogue for 1929 before me. At the same time he raised one eyebrow at a pretty little occasional table I had picked up at an auction sale. He tapped it.

"That was made," he said, "in 1925 for one Robinson Bey by Sayed Suliman – a poor carpenter – one who has since died. The wood is bad. The craftsmanship is bad. The bolish is not good. It cannot last. Soon," he murmured, becoming every moment more prophetically Russian, "the wood will crack – the white ant will feed on it – the table will fall into many, many tiny pieces. Gone! Finished! What, then, has been the use?"

"Let us speak," I said, under steely control, "of our new tea-table. I wish it to be – as we say in English – octagonal. That is, with eight sides."

The carpenter was much impressed. Momentarily he was silenced. Then he said: "That is possible. Why not? Eight sides. One, two, three, four . . . and so on. I am able to do whatever you say. Eight sides," he cried excitedly, "nine sides, ten sides, eleven sides –"

"Eight, I thank you, will be sufficient," I replied. I still minded about the occasional table.

"Then enough talk," said the carpenter agreeably.

I did not know whether he meant my talk or his, but he was making for his bicycle, so I said, "First, let us plan how high the table will be." He measured suddenly from his foot to his knee.

"There is a good height," he said, "What better?"

I didn't like to criticize the height of his knee from the ground, but said I thought it on the low side. He shrugged his shoulders and made another generous gesture.

"As you will," he said. "Say the height you will. I shall construct it." I had no time to say the height; he had his foot on the pedal.

"Tomorrow all will be settled and planned," he prophesied optimistically. "If you are not satisfied, then speak!"

I would have spoken; but no words sprang to mind.

"Once," he said, getting it in at last, "I made a tea-table for Sir Ball Biscuit. Sir Ball Biscuit," he said, his liquid eyes brimming with reproach, "was very well pleased." He rang the bell, and took the corner at an angle.

"I have not forgotten the paint!" he exclaimed, beaming, as he arrived inconveniently at lunch-time the following day. "I carry in my mind all that you say. You ask for your furniture to be painted yellow. I search the market. I go in at one shop. I go in at another. Sometimes they have green paint, blue paint, red paint . . ."

"White paint and black paint," I joined in.

"True," said the carpenter, very surprised "But where is the yellow paint? Late at night I find it."

He opened a tin, produced a brush, and painted strokes freely on our garden furniture. The colour revolted me.

"No, no!" I said. "That is mustard."

"It is not mustard," said the carpenter kindly "it is paint."

"The *colour*," I explained. "It is the colour of mustard. I wished for the colour of honey."

"Do we speak of food?" inquired the carpenter, always agreeable to changing the conversation.

"No," I said, "we speak of paint. I want a lighter paint."

"You mean white," said the carpenter.

"I do not. I mean yellow."

"The owner of the shop told me this paint was yellow paint, and he is a man I would trust with my life," the carpenter said, grandly.

"It is yellow," I agreed, "but it should be lighter, softer, paler . . ."

The carpenter had the well-known psychological defect of escaping from what he could not master.

"Have we not had enough talk of paint?" he said, and bicycled away.

When he appeared the next day in a laundered robe, his mood had changed.

"I have come for five pounds," he said.

"Five pounds! But you haven't started yet," I exclaimed.

"Your excellency," said the carpenter, "wants the best wood. Your excellency wants a tea-table with countless sides. Your excellency wants a paint which is not. I must therefore have money."

"A pound," I said.

"Five," said the carpenter.

The insidious climate, the sleepy sun-drenched garden, the monotonous birds, the fact that I had got everything ready to wash my hair – these are the things which influence decision. I gave him five pounds.

Not inexplicably, he so far has paid no further visit.

Whatever furniture and effects had been accumulated, all had to be transported in rackety old lorries from one end of the country to the other every two or three years. One wife noted ruefully that in seventeen years she had had seven moves. In view of these frequent transfers and the appalling roads it does now seem surprising that there was no government issue of basic furniture which could have been left in each house. (Any reader should by now be able to guess one of the reasons why this had not been effected). 'Every three years', wrote one wife whose sojourn in the country covered almost the whole period of these memoirs, 'I vowed to leave the furniture behind, neglect the new garden and live in the wilderness with basic packing cases. All over the country there must have been women making the same resolutions. But none of us escaped the urge to try to make each new station a home, however makeshift and temporary.'

✳

8 *Plagues*

Anyone from the West reading about the efforts of Moses and Aaron to leave Pharaoh's Egypt might idly wonder how the person responsible managed to think up so many diverse plagues. Anyone who had spent a week or two in Sudan would be more likely to wonder why he had stopped short at ten. Diseases attacking man and beast were legion: the vagaries of the climate were extreme if predictable; and the unpleasant members of the invertebrate kingdom both ubiquitous and uncountable.

Curiously, the horror of these small creatures was inversely proportionate to their medical consequences. Mosquitoes were a known and constant threat in most places and sandfly in some. Almost hand-sized spiders with thick black legs, bedbugs, undeviating columns of black ants and dragonfly-sized wasps had no long lasting physical effect, but a devastating psychological one, at least on women. Other creatures neither horrific nor dangerous, such as white ants, made up for it in nuisance value. There must surely have been *some* nice insects in the country but none has been recalled.

Even smaller than the sandfly were *nimitti*. They hovered in clouds within three hundred yards of the river in Khartoum and caused streaming eyes and a running nose, badly affecting anyone prone to asthma. They swarmed round lights so that between December and April it was impossible to sit out in a garden near the river, and almost impossible to work in even a closed office. Further north up the Nile there were two other types of *nimitti* which became a nuisance as early as October.

Anywhere in Sudan electric light or the light of Petromax lamps attracted from the seemingly peaceful void of the night a perpetual stream of dive-bombing, fluttering, flying creatures. To the unzoological it was a surprise to find that some of the more bizarre specimens had ever been invented. Cognoscenti were reminded that insects are the most successful class of the entire animal kingdom, comprising over half a million known species.

In the south where the insects were both more numerous and more medically dangerous, a portable square mosquito-net room-cum-tent was often used. Lamps had to be left outside and the resulting dim light within made both reading and sewing well-nigh impossible. Alternatively, part of the veranda could be enclosed in mosquito-wire. Where there was no veranda, a permanent mosquito-wired room or *namlia* was constructed and often used for sleeping in at night. Yet even that could not protect against every type of insect, as one wife found to her acute discomfort: 'One terrible night we both woke up on being bitten and, switching on the torch, we discovered a great column of soldier ants marching, quite undeterred, not only through the mosquito wire but through the nets as well.' Smaller black ants invariably proved a nuisance in the house and anything sweet had to be kept in bowls of water. These ants were difficult to see on the black quarry-tile floors, particularly at night in the very dim electric light. A certain wife was hoping to make an impression at the Palace Ball in a slinky black dress. Unfortunately its train swept up some ants and just as she was about to depart she had to dash back to the bedroom and pull everything off, completely spoiling her especially arranged hair-do. Far more of a menace in most houses were the so-called white ants, social insects with a caste system similar to that of ants but, scientifically speaking, they were pseudo-neuropterous termites, their eyeless workers devouring cellulose in any form with unbelievable rapidity, provided they could eat away in darkness.

They always left a paper-thin external skin intact which disguised their depredations. One couple, who thought they had brought out enough packets of Bromo to last them nine months, discovered when they went to take the first replacement that white ants had eaten the lot. The all-but-twelve hours of darkness were a satisfyingly happy time for these fast eaters. Before getting into bed the experienced made sure that no bedclothes touched the floor and that they had tucked their slippers under the mattress. If a dressing-gown slipped off the bed during the night, a gnawed remnant would be found in the morning. For this reason the legs of furniture stood in lids of paraffin when these white ants were prevalent. Some optimists who ignored this precaution had thereafter to prop their damaged furniture up on bricks.

Every wife in the service experienced the exasperating depredations of white ants in one place or another, but comparatively few suffered from (or were frank enough to write about) the scourge of bedbugs.

A Dinka cattle camp

One exception, a wife at Opari, was sent in 1933 to Juba hospital in an attempt to diagnose her recurrent bouts of fever. 'One night I realised something was biting me. I fumbled to light the *shamadan* outside my mosquito net. When at last it was lit I saw four lines of bedbugs advancing from the four posts of the net.' One is left wondering how she dealt with the predicament. Another wife felt that the bugs showed an unfair sexual discrimination. 'My husband was hardly ever bitten; it was invariably I who returned from a visit or tea-party with bites at the back of my knees. I was told it was not done for me to wear trousers but eventually I did, and saved myself further discomfort.'

That same wife recorded another experience.

'When we went on leave from Fasher to the Middle East in 1943 I took a large supply of Keating's and used it everywhere to good effect. Even so, at times I was still bitten. When we returned to Fasher I thought what bliss it would be to sleep undisturbed in my own bed under the glorious stars once more! Before long I felt an all too familiar sensation. My husband was already asleep so I decided not to complain. But it soon became too much for me so I woke him up. He thought I had bugs on the brain but he dutifully lit the lamp. There they all were, armies of them, a whole parade on the march from his bed to mine. We discovered next day that our *syce*, who acted as our night-watchman, had slept as instructed on our veranda while we were away. Instead of bringing his own bed he had just put his bedding roll on my husband's. In the end we had to burn that *anqarayb*'.

More disliked than bedbugs, because more frightening, were scorpions. It became an unconscious reflex action to shake out a shoe or slipper before ever putting it on. When a wife sighted a scorpion, she kept it carefully under surveillance, and shouted for servants to bring an implement. The creature could be despatched by one well-aimed blow, but servants in the excitement of the chase bashed and crashed with mounting whoops of joy and terror. Exactly the same thing happened when they tried to hit a snake. Often it turned out that they had in fact killed a poor harmless grass snake. To them, as to most people in England to this day, any snake was a snake. It is interesting how universally deep-rooted is the abhorrence of snakes, from the Garden of Eden story onward. A wife in Kassala felt the phobia in 1940. When told to go to a deep ravine in the event of an Italian air raid, she went to inspect the place, 'saw at least a dozen snakes in five minutes', and declared that no Italian bomber would make her go there. Fortunately nobody called her bluff.

Even more feared in the Sudan than snakes and scorpions were rabid dogs. Apart from the risk of death, the antidote of twenty-four injections in the wall of the stomach proved excruciatingly painful. 'When my husband was in Khartoum North he was bitten by a dog which might have been rabid. So he had to go to hospital every morning for the necessary twenty-four anti-rabies injections. By the twentieth day the sister had to start injecting in a place she had already used; the result was extremely painful. My husband somehow managed to bear three more injections but then both he and the sister agreed to stop before the last.' Most people had the sense not to keep dogs, but some ignored the risk. So many stray dogs ran loose that certain parents made a point of keeping their gate shut if they had small children, reversing the practice in nearby Kenya, where the gate was kept shut to keep the fierce dog *in*.

Locusts, one of the original ten plagues, could have been expected. Some years they invaded and then for some years they never came. One method of controlling them was to locate the wingless hoppers somewhere in the desert across the Red Sea and poison them from a plane with Gammexane. A single locust was not in itself repellent; it had the fascination of any grasshopper with its ingeniously-shaped overlapping scales and beautiful markings on the hopping leg. Locusts, like so many other insects out there, overwhelmed and daunted the wives with their stupendous and infinite number.

This feeling is conveyed by a wife who encountered locusts in Wad Medani just before the War:
'They were far more alarming than either *habubs* or violent thunderstorms. The sky went completely dark and millions of locusts came in thick clouds. They covered absolutely everything, not only outside, where anything green was devoured, but all the doors, walls, and floors inside. It took several days before we managed to brush the last one out of the house.'

Another plague, the ninth in the Biblical series, was the dust-storm or *habub* which 'caused darkness over the land of Egypt, a darkness which may be felt.' (A recent speculation is that this 'darkness' was caused by the ash fall-out from the volcanic eruption that destroyed Knossos.) Whichever cause is preferred it does not alter the fact that the Old Testament came frequently to life in twentieth-century Sudan. The following description amplifies the earlier one in the Bible:

'Dust-storms were the scourge of the summer months before the rains came. A strong, hot, dust-laden wind filled the air so thick with dust and sand that everything was blotted out.' Even glass in the windows did not keep out this sand: 'I remember the darkening skies, the menacing thick brown cloud approaching, the preliminary gusts of wind, crashing doors and windows which sent servants round quickly shutting up the house. Then with the full blast of the storm

A family on the move in Darfur

Abdim's storks nesting in central Sudan village

came inky blackness. Birds crashed against the lighted windows, sand forced itself through every crack so that inside the house absolutely every surface was covered with a layer of it, while our own skins darkened with sweaty dust. Then, as quickly as it came, the storm passed and daylight returned. The servants started cleaning up with frantic flapping of dusters and swishing brooms.'

It was more annoying when the *habub* started in the middle of the night for then all the bedding had to be quickly rolled up and taken into the house. Here, with all the shutters tightly closed, the rest of the night was sure to be too hot and stuffy to allow any sleep.

Familiarity made the *habub* less terrifying and its aftermath less dismaying. Once their season was over there was blissful relief until the next year. In Tokar, however, near the eastern coast a wind blew all the time.

'A strong wind blew relentlessly, threatening to submerge buildings, roads and the narrow-gauge railway to the coast. The sand penetrated every nook and cranny. It even managed to force its way between some Spode dessert plates and to this day there is dust under the glaze. Our dining-room table had drawers into which we put our plates of food, closing them between each mouthful. At certain times of the year we tied a rope between our house and the office so that my husband would not get lost on the way.

Occasionally we went to the coast and stayed in the resthouse over the Police post and court room. If the wind dropped it was pleasant to sit out on the roof. One evening when the *sufragi* was bringing up a tray set for our small son's supper, an unexpectedly strong gust of wind swept up and removed everything from the tray; plates, knives, spoons and boiled egg departed over the horizon.'

As well as these periodic trials, the ever-present discomfort of great heat had to be endured. It produced a distressing malaise that is difficult to convey. For some it brought persistent prickly heat that could irritate to screaming point. Always the heat had an enervating effect, on locals and foreigners alike, with the possible exception of a few Scots. Most wives preferred the dry heat of the north, even though it made them feel brittle, to the high humidity of the south.

One wife actually recorded an April temperature in her house in Wad Medani of 94°F at breakfast-time and then, even though the house had been shut up, 104°F by midday. Wives often gauged the heat by the nature of baths they took during the day. In Khartoum, for a blissful six weeks or so around Christmas, they welcomed a hot bath in the evening. After that it did not matter so much if the servants had made the water only tepid. Gradually the number of cold baths increased to four; one on waking if it had been a really stuffy night, a second after riding or walking before breakfast, a third after the siesta and then the usual evening bath. This cooling programme was of course possible only in Khartoum and centres with piped water. Nobody missed showers, which would have been such a perfect answer, because they were not at that time in general use at home.

In the hotter months, even though the sun disappeared with its usual rapidity around six o'clock, the ground continued to reflect the heat. One D.C. in Rashad had (untypically) attempted to improve matters by building a raised platform to catch the breeze a little distance from the house, on the same principle used, on a very much grander scale, for the mis-named 'hanging' gardens in Babylon, which were in effect a construction of no fewer than seven stories. Nebuchadnezzar had them built in 650 BC for his wife, not only to catch the breeze but also because she pined for the greenery of her native land. This was as understandable to anyone in Sudan as was the Persians' ancient belief that Heaven must be an irrigated garden or 'paradise'.

Wives in stations on or near the Nile could enjoy the soothing and cooling effect of irrigated greenery and water. But wherever their station, some women tolerated the heat better than others, either for physical or mental reasons. Did some find the country unbearable because they had recurrent dysentery? Or did they have recurring ills and ailments because they disliked the climate, the conditions and the insects?

9 *The Domestic Staff*

Sudanese servants, no matter whether they came from north or south, had a remarkable ability to learn quickly about strange foreign customs and ways. For instance, eating neatly with their fingers they nevertheless mastered and laid correctly our formidable array of cutlery. Of the whole canteen they particularly prized fish knives and forks which they considered a sign of status. Therefore if their master chose to entertain and owned no fish knives, these would be borrowed from next door. They also borrowed other items to ensure prestige, invariably without the knowledge of the owner. At a dinner party in Khartoum a wife 'was intrigued to notice that our hostess had exactly the same coffee service that we had. Only next day did I discover that it *was* ours.'

This zeal to please and to do the best for the house went with a cheerful willingness and a natural courtesy. These qualities combined with their training by innumerable *sitts* (ladies) gained for Sudanese servants the reputation of being better at their job than other Middle-Eastern nationals. From 1939 onwards they enjoyed such prestige that Americans and others whisked them off to Egypt; later on many found their own way to Arabia and comparative wealth.

Before that time, families never experienced any difficulty in finding Sudanese willing to become servants. Although their wages sound very low today, to compensate for this they had better food, clothes and living conditions than their relatives and friends. Fortunately the Muslims did not suffer from the rigid caste system enforced by Hindus in India, where a sweeper always remained a sweeper. The lowliest cook's boy, called a *marmiton,* could in due course work his way up to being the cook and having his own slave; or he could even become the chief servant, the *sufragi*, who ran the house. 'In Fasher our *marmiton* started his career as my husband's golf-caddie and on being translated to our kitchen soon became a good cook: he was intelligent and had a real flair for cooking. Later, when he came to Khartoum with us, he attended English classes. When we left the country he became the cook in the American Embassy.'

By tradition the best servants came from Dongola in the north, the chief servants in the Palace being self-perpetuating *Dongolawis*. They left their families in little mud houses beside the Nile, each with one or two date palms, their only other source of income, but would return once a year bearing what money they had managed to save.

In 1937 an A.D.C. in the south was paying his Northern cook £E 3.00, the Southern *sufragi* £E 2.00, and their respective number twos fifty piastres each, making a total of £E 6.00 a month out of his salary of £E 40.00. Had he been in an area where it was possible to keep horses, he would have been employing a *syce* and several stable boys as well, thus paying out a quarter of his monthly salary on wages.

The majority of servants were selected in Khartoum by an established system.

'Before leaving Khartoum for El Obeid in 1945 we had to find some servants. News of our intention soon spread and about thirty applicants came to see us in the house where we were staying. Some undoubtedly friends or relations of our host's servants. Each had a record book containing his photo, his fingerprints and also the names of his previous employers. Some of the references they produced were good, some were not, but both were presented with pride, presumably because they had never been translated. We eventually chose Abbas. He looked neat and cheerful. We didn't know till later that he had a mania for folding things. Any clothes I left on my chair were carefully folded and put out in a line. He not only folded my husband's clothes too but also ironed his pyjamas every morning.'

Finding a replacement servant in an out-station was quite another matter. There were unlikely to be any experienced servants from which to choose. Possible applicants came from the local tribe, be it Nuer, Zande or Nuba. They were not necessarily less intelligent than the Northerners but at the outset they would probably know even less Arabic than the *sitt* herself. More often than not the selection was made by one of the existing servants.

'When I first went out in 1945 my husband persuaded his *sufragi* to become the cook as he had a smattering of English which would help in my daily transactions with him. It certainly did. After our first leave Ahmed asked to go back to being a *sufragi* again because he found the cookhouse too hot. He said he had found a chap called Ali who was willing to learn to cook and whom he would teach. Ali had

Zande with a harp

73

a smiling face but I noticed that his teeth were ground down almost flat. "Yes, of course" explained my husband, "he is a Zande", adding as if for further recommendation, "they were cannibals." The last reported incident of cannibalism had been in 1930 and nobody less ferocious and man-eating than Ali could be imagined. He did strike me as rather an odd choice for our cook though. Ali was gentle, willing and subservient – which was one reason why our *sufragi* had chosen him – and stayed with us through many culinary disasters until we were transferred north.'

Good servants usually did not leave unless for some misdemeanour and then the parting was often more in sorrow than in anger. 'Abbas [who folded clothes so neatly] was one of the best servants we ever had. We trusted him absolutely. One day a guest told us that he had lost some money in our house and that it had happened before. Sadly it was proved that Abbas had taken it, so he had to go.' In his defence it can be said that he probably would not have stolen from his master. In 1931 another couple unwillingly lost a very good *sufragi* because 'he was found to be in possession of hashish, cannabis.' Of course he had to be tried and went to prison. One of my husband's jobs at the time was the prevention of drug trafficking.'

Zande sowing grain

74

A different cause for a servant's departure could be the arrival of a wife. In a bachelor establishment a *sufragi* not only ran the other servants but could run the bachelor as well. As an independent factotum he would have become accustomed not only to his standing but to his perks and would not like to have either of them reduced, certainly not by a mere interfering *sitt*. One wife remembered that 'during my first year in the Sudan both the cook and the *sufragi* left as they both preferred to work for bachelors.' This was not the inevitable outcome of a wife's arrival; it would vary according to the personalities of the two individuals concerned. A newly-arrived bride in 1932 wrote, 'I was introduced to my husband's *sufragi*/cook who was a dear old Arab called Tahir. He was my husband's very first servant and had been with him for five years. He now adopted me, and only his ill health six years later put an end to our happy relationship.'

Junior servants left more often, frequently for promotion in another household. Any servant, especially the most senior, enjoyed a sense of promotion and increase of prestige with each promotion of his employer. For each grade in the Sudan Political Service there was an expected number of servants imposed by the *sufragi* whose *sharaf* (pride) would be upset were they not, on master's promotion, able to have more servants to control, as well as an automatic rise in salary. Only sometimes did promotion mean more entertaining, more visitors and a larger house. An augmented staff occurred irrespectively.

The *sufragi* was the major-domo in any household. No stage costume could make him look more impressive. He wore an impeccably white *imma* (turban) on his head giving him added height, a flowing floor-length *qaftan* (robe) and round his waist a coloured *cummerbund*. Wives had scope to exercise their artistic talent in the choice of material, or their ingenuity in making up this *cummerbund*; and some, in the same spirit of one-upmanship, further embellished the result with an embroidered province badge. In the early days, when the wife's tour lasted only a matter of months, the *sufragi* would continue to run the house, communicating only with his master and ignoring the wife. As an experienced servant of a top official he would do little menial work himself, apart from handing round drinks and waiting at table where he picked up all the news, rarely letting on how much English he knew. The best *sufragi* closely resembled the traditional English butler. A young wife in 1941 corroborates this. 'The Governor's *sufragi* was the personification of impressive dignity. He thought little of me and I felt knee-high in his presence. The first time I stood in for the Governor's wife, who was in England, I poured nervously from the silver teapot, forgetting to use the silver tea-strainer. Kerar moved behind me and with enormous dignity and disdain picked up the strainer and placed it in the next cup.'

As regards the smooth running of his house, that Governor would not have missed his wife's presence. A good and reliable *sufragi* proved an invaluable asset. Some, while the wife remained in residence, were clever and tactful enough to let her assume she had sole charge. 'I was told that I must make sure to hide the store-room key carefully every day so I used to vary the place as much as possible. Once I couldn't remember where I had hidden it the day before. Eventually I had to admit to Ahmed that I had lost the key. "I know where it is *sa'at es sitt* (your excellency the lady)," he replied and went straight to my *terai*, where he picked the key out from the ribbon round the crown. I thought I had always been so careful to hide it while no-one was looking.'

In general the servants saw and heard a good deal more than either side chose to admit. No Northerner would confess to peeping, but a less sophisticated Southerner saw no need to dissemble. 'As we were finishing our siesta our Latuka servant pushed open the door and carried in our tea on a tray. I hardly had time to pull up the sheet. "How many times have I told you to knock before coming into our bedroom" I cried angrily. "That's all right, *sa'at es sitt*" he answered soothingly, "I always look through the keyhole before I enter."'

All the hard and laborious work in a house fell to the 'number two' boy who, besides cleaning the house, moving the furniture out and in, also did the washing. There was never a problem about drying. A washed petticoat was ready to put on in ten minutes and babies' nappies did not take much longer. Cold water, bar soap and a heavy cumbersome, unpredictable charcoal iron made the rest of the process more arduous. 'Our household washing was done in a large oversize tin washing-up bowl on the ground. Considering the primitive equipment the results were remarkably good. The use of Reckitt's blue was a tradition passed down from an earlier generation of wives. It was still being used by Sudanese servants in 1948 long after it had become almost non-existent in England. As a result the sheets used to end up a queer grey colour. The heavy charcoal flat-iron required skill and expertise to use and it was surprising that so few items were scorched. Only occasionally did we find little burn holes here and there where small pieces of red-hot charcoal had dropped out.'

❋　❋　❋

Next to the *sufragi* in status, but of equal importance, came the cook. He headed as it were a separate department and communicated directly with the *sitt*. Invariably in the early days, but not so frequently after the war, he had his own 'plumber's mate', called the *marmiton*. The cook-house, always some distance from the house because of the danger of

76

fire when both buildings were thatched, and the area around it, tended to be the servants' 'common room'. All the cooking took place on an old-fashioned, wood-burning kitchen range. In out-stations the cook had no sink or running water; most of the preparation of food and all the washing up was done on the ground outside. As in smart restaurants the world over, the less that was known of this stage of the meal, the better for everyone's equanimity. Perhaps a few wives regularly inspected the cook-house but this wife's confession speaks for the majority: 'in all my years out there, I never once went into it, partly through nervousness and partly because it would have felt like prying into the servants' quarters.'

How the cooks managed to do as well as they did on those antiquated ranges remains a mystery. In spite of the climate most people habitually had three cooked meals a day. In a senior official's house after the war cereals at breakfast were followed by fish in some form, then by eggs or sausages as individually ordered from the *sufragi*. The final meal consisted of a many-course dinner which could be called up, peremptorily, at any moment between half-past-eight and ten. Apparently one cook did equally well on a barge. 'My first home in Western Nuer District in 1943 was on a barge pushed by a Nile steamer. It was surprising what excellent meals our cook could prepare on the lower deck in a little kitchen, no more than four foot square and always filled with smoke. We had crocodile-tail steaks which looked like chicken but tasted fishy; wild turkey stuffed with elephant's heart, the best stuffing I have ever had; buffalo soup, like strong beef tea, and home-made biscuits and cheese. Once, when he fell ill, I tried to do the supper but, after several attempts at various dishes, I finally produced only hot milk and whisky.'

Showing such prowess, cooks excelled even on trek where they were still expected to produce the usual three-course dinner, 'even when conditions became so difficult as to be impossible.' Another wife remembers: 'on one trek the lorry stuck deep in mud. All around the water lay in pools but a little distance away there was a small rise and a dry island. I waded to this followed by a policeman carrying a camp chair and the cook carrying his cook box. While the others struggled to free the lorry, evening became night so, by the light of a lantern, I sat and knitted. Later on the cook somehow produced the usual meal.' A second anecdote concerns a trek in 1935. 'Our cook did not come with us on this trek but a seventeen-year-old boy, Abd el-Kerim, surprised us by being unbelievably swift and efficient. From behind an anthill he produced the best omelette I have ever tasted, and I include the Dorchester, Claridge's and the Savoy.'

The *sitt* commonly interviewed the cook every morning to record what had been spent in the *suq* the day before and then to order the

Zande mother

78

meals for the ensuing day. This was difficult for the new wife, not only linguistically but because invariably she had had no experience of dealing with servants herself before coming out. Not infrequently wives would feel shy and diffident, reluctant to query anything in the *suq* bill. Then, according to the extent of her moral courage, or how well she felt that day, the wife might investigate the price of one or two items. The cook inevitably had a reasonable excuse for the unreasonable. But the *sitt*'s scrutiny remained salutary (as well as courageous) and helped to keep the weekly bill down. Occasionally persistence could bring dismissal. 'Our cook had been quite good so far but now in Wau he became rather truculent. He insisted that he needed a *ras* and a half (over a kilogramme) of sugar and also three bars of soap a day. So we parted company.'

This cook had probably up till then been working only for bachelors, who rarely bothered to look into the food bill and could be easily hoodwinked, as this wife records.

'Until the roads were open after the rains and we could return to our own house in Waat, we lived next to the D.C. in Fangak. We used to dine with each other frequently. Whenever we dined with him on a Thursday he apologised for the fact that there was no meat left – or so his servant had said. I was surprised because we usually had enough meat and there were two of us. A bull would be killed on a Friday and each household allowed a certain amount. We bought two and a half *okes*, an *oke* being about a kilogram. So I asked the D.C. how much meat he usually had. He didn't know. When he looked into it later he discovered that his servant had been buying ten okes. He realised that he couldn't possibly have consumed nearly thirty pounds of meat in a week, even though he entertained us some nights. No wonder servants disliked it when their master married!'

After dealing with the *suq* bill there followed the arduous task of arranging the day's menu, a job more difficult than it sounds. 'I couldn't cook in English let alone Arabic when I first went out. I would laboriously translate a recipe word by word using Hillelson's invaluable *Sudan Arabic*. Unfortunately, good as he was in most respects, Hillelson had evidently never had to 'fold' in an egg, or 'simmer' a dish and was as useless as I at converting 'Regulo 4' or 'gas mark three' into an equivalent for the erratic old wood-burning stove.'

Needless to say, many a slip between the *sitt* and the lip resulted from the all too frequent misunderstandings. Amusing in retrospect, wives often found such disasters frustrating at the time.

'One day I went to great trouble to explain to our new and rather dumb Zande cook how to make a really good soup stock instead of the thin tea-like water he tended to produce. "Cook the meat with onions and vegetables, very slowly, then after a time take it off the hob and pour it through a *musfah* (sieve)". We were looking forward to some tasty soup that evening. Imagine my chagrin when the soup tasted even worse than usual. Next morning I said to Ali, "What happened to the soup? Didn't you put onions with the meat?" "Yes, *sa'at es-sitt*, I did exactly as you said. I poured it through the sieve but all that was left were bones and the onion skins and they did not look good to eat." "But Ali, didn't you put anything *under* the sieve?" "No, *sa'at es-sitt* he replied solemnly "you never told me to." And he was quite right. I hadn't. So I had been pretty dumb too. Ali obviously thought it was entirely my fault that the stock had been poured into the sand, so I said no more.'

Another wife encountered similar difficulties when trying to arrange a dinner party. Her account appeared in *Punch* in 1948, and is reproduced by permission of *Punch*.

When the cook entered the room his expression combined hostility with a slight touch of jaundice, and his gait a modest though quite misplaced confidence in his own talent. We said "good morning," and though there seemed little chance of improving the atmosphere, I commended him for his cake the day before. In fluent Arabic I said that it had been nearly right (better, anyhow, than before – more or less) at last. More could not have been said, since the whole interior had looked (though not tasted) like marzipan.

He seemed indifferent.

"To God be the thanks," he said, raising one eyebrow.

I went on swiftly: "Today there will be four people to dinner."

He looked seriously displeased. He thought a little. "Two, then," he concluded in a kind of wishful thinking, "are coming. Two guests. That will be four altogether."

"No," I said; "four are coming. Four guests."

"Therefore," said the cook, falling back on some obscure mathematics of his own, "there will be four more and two less."

"I mean," I said, "that there will be six altogether."

"Is that so?" he asked coldly.

There was a pause. I went on to the next point. "Where is today?" I asked briskly, but with a slight disregard for minor points of grammar.

"How," said the cook.

It did not seem in any way a comprehensive answer. Casting my mind over a chapter on adverbs I started again.

What is there today?" I asked. "Is there any fish?"

He became suddenly voluble.

"Fish!" he exclaimed. "If there is fish in the suk I shall bring it. But if there is no fish, it is impossible I should bring it. Sometimes there is fish; sometimes there is no fish. None in the canals, none in the wadi, none in the rivers, even in the sea, if it is not the proper season —"

"Should there be fish," I said, keeping my head, "I should like it fried."

"If the fish is to be fried one must first make of the bread extremely small pieces," said the cook, in the tone of one suggesting an insuperable difficulty.

I said curtly "Yes, one must."

"Very well, then," said the cook, resigned to this piece of unnecessary trouble. "There is also meat."

"What kind?"

"A sheep – a rosta!" he cried, graphically illustrating the cut on his own anatomy.

"Then we will have roast mutton and mint sauce."

"Good!" said the cook, "there is no mint."

"No mint in the suk?"

"By God," said the cook passionately, "if there is mint in the suk, I will buy it; but if there is not mint in the suk, how is it possible for me to buy it? Your Excellency knows that I am a magnificent cook," he went on frankly, "and the buying of the mint is on my own head. It may be found in the suk; it may not be found –"

"If it is found in the suk, buy it!" I shouted back, and went on rapidly: "For a sweet, beat the cream strongly and add to it the fruit from a bottle which I will presently give you."

"As for the cream," he said, this time in a tone of extreme reasonableness, "it may take, or it may not take. I may beat the cream and it may become stiff; again I may beat it and it may not become stiff – only by God's will shall it become stiff."

There was no answer to such a fatalistic attitude about the cream, and the cook, bored with all this talk of food, said suddenly: "Your Excellency, I should like a watch."

"A what?" I said, startled.

"A time – an hour – a watch! Tick-tick," he explained, making himself clear.

"I will see."

"One," he persisted, "that encircles my wrist."

"We speak," I said, "of lunch. We will have cold ham and fruit salad and that is all."

He went to the door. At the door he turned. "Let not the watch," he said, "be from the store here, for they are cheap. Better than that can be obtained elsewhere."

"I have said, 'We will see'," I replied in tones of ice.

"If," he finally concluded, "you cannot find one to encircle the wrist, I will accept one that hangs from a chain."

He went out, closing the door firmly behind him.

That typified exchanges prior to any ordinary dinner party. Misunderstandings and consequent disasters occurred even more often when a prestigious guest was due and both the cook and the *sitt* hoped to produce something impressive. In 1928 the Governor-General was visiting a large tribal gathering in Kassala and a young wife 'had to give a dinner party for His Excellency. When the sweet course was served, supposedly trifle, to my horror it was in two dishes, cake in one, custard in the other.' A year or two later a D.C.'s wife had to entertain their Governor in Upper Nile Province. For the occasion the servants had been issued with brand new white *laus* (a small tablecloth knotted over one shoulder.) 'They looked very smart as they handed round the soup. Unfortunately there was then a tremendous downpour of rain. The servants did not want to get their precious new *laus* wet coming across from the cookhouse, so when they arrived to serve the fish they arrived as Mother Nature made them.'

For many wives, entertaining always proved an anxiety, no matter how long they had been in the country. Others, with a different temperament, or senior enough to be able to afford a good and experienced cook, would order nonchalantly for large parties as if in Hever Castle. 'In Darfur the Governor's Christmas party ran on lines laid down by years of repetition. I had little to do beyond telling the cook that there would be forty to dinner and sixty to the following supper, the increase due to some members of the R.A.F. and U.S.A.F. then being off duty. On being told of this daunting assignment the cook imperturbably replied "There is no objection".'

What kind of food appeared at these parties and from where did it come? Three sources existed: local produce, imported items from a very limited number of shops, and provisions brought out from home.

Local meat presented no problem; it just tended to be tough as it had to be eaten at once. In general, scraggy sheep and even scraggier chickens abounded. Neither tasted of very much when used with fresh cooking fat; both tasted disgusting when it was bad. There were plenty of tiny eggs and most places, except for those in a tsetse fly area, had milk. Very often the local shaikh would lend a cow, only too thankful to have it properly fed for a while. The milk, arriving in any container that happened to be handy, was neither tuberculin-tested nor particularly clean. It often had hairs in it, much to the displeasure of the children, but with certain exceptions it usually tasted all right. 'I once complained that the milk had a very odd taste. Only then did I discover that the Nuer had a habit of mixing cow's urine with the milk in order to increase their salt intake. This was no doubt sensible as far as they were concerned but I decided I preferred to take my salt in other ways.'

A night watchman

There were one or two Government fruit gardens which could be productive for short periods but for the majority of wives fresh fruit and vegetables constituted a real problem for most of the year. 'Small fresh limes could be found quite often. The local Sudanese commonly thought that the astounding ability of white men to do without a woman was the result of drinking lime juice, either fresh or 'Rose's'. I can remember on my first visit to Dueim in 1928 seeing oranges on the sideboard and feeling I could hardly bear to wait to be offered one. At that time our cook, Abdullahi, was a master of everything except cooking. He was a distant cousin of el Sayyid Sir Abd el-Rahman, one of the two religious leaders, a connection ensuring us a warm welcome from all the locals in the Blue and White Nile Provinces, and also some perks. Abdullahi arranged with his brother on the post boat to hand across some butter each time he passed, another cousin sent vegetables and some other relative sent bread.'

To a newcomer it came as a surprise to find Greek merchants' shops in so many out-of-the-way places in the Sudan. In fact the Greeks had been in Khartoum in Gordon's time and some had provisioned Kitchener's army on its march south in the 1890s. They, with additional relatives and friends, had remained in the country ever since. Some had originally intended to return home when they became rich and prosperous; neither aim was universally achieved and a Greek wife in Talodi, for example, waited in vain. In Khartoum there were also Armenian and Syrian traders, of whom, in the provision line, Morhig's was the 'Harrods'. Newcomers made use of this shop on arrival and remained customers for the rest of their years in the Sudan. 'It was quite a business ordering goods from Khartoum in 1928 because, before there were *suq* lorries, everything had to come to Dueim on the fortnightly post boat.'

To supplement the items stocked by these traders, people before the War brought out supplies from home. A wife wrote of the nineteen-twenties, 'we bought out as much tinned stuff as our cash and small credit would allow. I remember once I had far too much lime-juice, Lux soap and Enos fruit salts. At Christmas relatives sent marvellous hampers containing tinned grouse, Stilton cheese, a huge cake, crystallised fruits (most of which had melted) and dozens of other small items.'

During the War and for some years afterwards many basic necessities disappeared, the most missed being white flour and potatoes. Tea and sugar were also rationed as at home. When the tea ran out, as it frequently did because the servants liked it, there was little joy in a cup of cocoa on a hot summer's afternoon. Nor was local flour any substitute, even on the rare occasions when it contained no weevils. 'At one feast day our servants gave us some buns made from local flour with rancid fat. We found them very difficult to eat. Every day they were carefully produced for tea. I used to smuggle two out to the loo and cover them with sand. Still they appeared; so I asked a number of people to tea whom I took into my confidence, and that meant I could get rid of all the rest of the buns in the same way on one day without offending the servants.'

This was was not being unusually fastidious. A visitor staying with the Commissioner of Port Sudan in the late nineteen-forties remarked that his bread was worse than any he had eaten as a prisoner-of-war. Because of the food shortages, one or two couples took a pride in living entirely off local produce. The majority thought them eccentric. Nor did the Sudanese cooks necessarily appreciate the effort.

'Being a Scotsman, A. had to have his salted porridge every morning regardless of the temperature outside. When oatmeal was not available we had a delicious porridge made from local *dukhn* (millet). When the oatmeal became available again back came the usual porridge. Our dear old cook absolutely refused to give us *dukhn* porridge again. It took me a little time to discover why. Apparently his sharp-tongued wife taunted him with being the great Commissioner of Port Sudan's chef but cooking food fit only for servants. So when we wanted *dukhn* porridge I had to cook it myself.'

Because of this and many other almost daily vexations, not to mention the servants' own recurring personal problems, often about a loan for a watch, a gold tooth or a wife, many women felt relief on going home on leave, to be free of it all for a time. Absence had its normal effect. During the leave presents were bought for all servants and on return there was genuine pleasure on both sides, even though the reunion was accompanied by a catalogue of mishaps – this plant had died, that animal was lame, the other eaten by a hyaena, this object had disappeared and the other ruined by rain coming through a leak . . . Instances of long service and appreciated loyalty have been recorded. 'Our cook and our *sufragi* remained with us all the sixteen years of our time in the Sudan. They became part of the family.' 'Daldun stayed with us the rest of our eleven years, during which he became the mainstay of our household and a much-loved friend to our children.' Another instance of a reciprocated relationship occurred when a certain Governor retired: there on the station platform, along with his jovial well-wishing friends, stood his weeping *sufragi*.

❋

10 *Trekking*

There is a perfectly good Arabic word *safar* for a journey (from which derives the Swahili *safari*) but for some reason so far unexplained, every Briton in the Sudan used the word 'trek'. This word might have come, as did the Penal Code, from the Indian Civil Service. But it did not: in India members of the I.C.S. habitually spoke of 'going on tour' around their districts and provinces.

The Dutch word trek came to Sudan from South Africa, where it specifically referred to travelling by an ox-drawn wagon. In Sudan, water was brought to houses in various contraptions often drawn by an ox but no record has been found of any person travelling by such means. A probable supposition is that some influential military gentleman travelling up north from the Boer War introduced the term.

Members of the Political Service, during their early years in the country, tended to spend at least half of their time on trek. This was not surprising as, although the size and extent of districts varied considerably over the whole country, the Eastern Jebels District for instance covered an area the size of Palestine. Apart from trying major court cases and explaining Government policy to local leaders throughout their area, D.C.s liaised with agricultural and veterinary officers and either together or independently supervised the building of dams, *hafars* and wells, the planting of trees against erosion and all the other jobs normally controlled by a County Council in Britain.

Trekking could be by camel, paddle-steamer, pony, lorry or by foot. In certain areas in the south, where tsetse-fly precluded the use of ponies, men covered many miles by bicycle before the days of motor transport. The type of transport used was dictated by the effect of the the rainfall on and over the differing terrains, because this affected the type and availability of roads.

A road in Darfur

In the sandy north it rained on only two or three days in the year, if at all. In the Khartoum–Port Sudan belt, six whole inches fell between July and September. The next latitude band going southward bene-fited from an annual rainfall comparable to London's twenty-four inches. By the time Malakal was reached, the rainfall had increased to thirty-four inches and the rainy season to the six months from May to October inclusive. The clay 'cotton soil' in the central southern plain, once flooded, became impossible for motor transport. That was the reason why many of the districts in this area were closed to women dur-ing the rains. In the event of illness it would have been impossible either to move out the ailing wife or to bring in medical help quickly. This restriction did not apply in the southernmost districts for here, despite high equatorial rainfall, the roads remained passable owing to the good draining quality of the ironstone.

The word 'road' in Sudan may be understood as a euphemism. Out-side and beyond the main centres, no roads comparable to those in Bri-tain existed. Routes taken went from A to B through, over or around any natural object in the way. No one in their senses in Britain would dream of driving a lorry from steeple to steeple across ditches, through hedges and around copses; but that happened in Sudan. Apart from avoiding strips of cultivation, a 'road' could and did traverse almost any

87

type of terrain. The lorries, once pointed in the right direction went chugging and jolting doggedly along, perhaps at ten or even twenty miles an hour. Small wonder that a wife once found to her dismay that the continuous friction had ruined her brand new Aertex shirt after only one day's travelling. 'The material over the shoulder blades had just worn away'. This was one reason perhaps why men were sensible enough to wear hot but tough khaki drill.

Even on comparatively good and smooth ironstone roads in the south there could be the hazard of unseen elephant droppings, dried as hard as stone and painful to bump over. The driver also had to keep a sharp look out for old ebony roots capable of splintering and shredding any tyre to pieces.

At intervals along most roads there were 'Irish bridges' which were meant to help the lorry down into, and up out of, any large ditch or wider *khur*. After the first bank had been negotiated safely, the graded incline up the other side often proved, on closer inspection, to have been damaged. The knowledge that the tribe responsible for the upkeep would ultimately receive a bad mark for this lapse did not help

A road near the Ethiopian frontier south east of Malakal

88

the passengers on the lorry, who perforce had to set to on lengthy repairs.

In the dry weather this presented no more than a hot and frustrating delay, but during the rains it could be a matter of anxiety or even danger. These rivers, dry for months, would fill with flood water which would rush down like the Severn Bore in a matter of minutes. One agriculturist, whose vehicle broke down in a *khur* after the start of the rains and who failed to get the engine started again in time, lost all his papers and many of his belongings.

Every Sudanese always carried bits of wire and string with him to repair any electrical or other fault; exactly how, no mechanically unsophisticated European wife ever knew. After the War, many of the lorries had rattled to bits, so an issue of brand new ones raised great expectations. They looked and promised to be very superior. Unfortunately they overheated with maddening frequency and their engines took ages to cool down. It later transpired that they were a war surplus specifically made for use in Canada and so had no efficient cooling system. In these and other lorries the extreme heat would vaporise the petrol, causing an air lock. The unfortunate driver had then to blow down into the petrol tank.

Apart from the mechanical vagaries of the transport, punctures were a dreaded trial and tribulation. They usually occurred at the hottest part of the day, at the most awkward moment on the trek, and in the most desolate of places. On some of these occasions a wife's morale could sink to an artesian depth and many a wife must then have vowed to herself not to go on trek next time. But of necessity she usually did: partly because the husband needed the servants and partly because the alternative must have been a sentence of solitary confinement and utter boredom. Only if the husband were more senior and had more servants, or if there were children to consider, would a wife opt to stay behind.

Whereas the men on trek always had more than enough to do, the wives during the heat of the day had to resort to sewing, sketching or reading. For them the worst result of an unforeseen delay or an extra two or three days on trek could be a shortage of reading material. 'I was already halfway through my last book so, in an attempt to make it last, I rationed myself to not more than ten pages an hour'. On another occasion a more embarrassing shortage was a diminishing supply of toilet paper, accentuated by one of the couple having an attack of dysentery. Only some of the major or minor disasters on trek seemed amusing in retrospect. A few have been recalled by a wife then stationed at Tonj in the south:

'Once we had a puncture about three o'clock when it was terribly hot, with absolutely no shade anywhere. As this should have been our last day on trek, we had very little water with us and found out that we were about five miles from a possible supply. Luckily the puncture was mended in about an hour and we set off again. We had hardly been going for twenty minutes when the tyre went again, this time for good. A puncture earlier on in the trek had left us without a spare so now it was a matter of trying to mend the valve of a very old discarded inner tube. We then managed to limp to a rest-house and sent off a runner to Tonj, fifty miles away.

After nineteen days on trek we had been so looking forward to a nice cold drink from the ice chest, to a comfortable bed to sleep on at home, and to some fresh fruit and vegetables. All our hopes were dashed to the ground. To make matters worse neither of us had anything to do and the rest-house turned out to be bat-ridden. We passed the time next afternoon by shooting at some of the bats with a .22. Luckily help arrived the next morning (the runner must have had winged feet) so we had had to spend only two nights there.

On another occasion that year we were crossing one of the grassy plains on a ramp built up above flood level when the lorry came to an abrupt standstill with a perilous list to one side. It was midday and a scorching wind was blowing dust into our faces. We hurriedly got out, to find that one of the back wheels had gone right through a badly-made bridge. For once we were grateful for the extra chaps who invariably managed to climb aboard just as our lorry set off.

Trying to lift the lorry, heavily loaded with some two tons of luggage, was both dangerous and difficult. Eventually the whole weight of the lorry rested on just one pole placed on the edge of a brick. We were ready to drive away. The lorry started with a jerk. Some stones and earth from the mended bridge pattered to the ground. The lorry paused ominously on the brink and then lurched forward again just as our reinforcements fell in.

After that hot and sweaty incident, we were greatly relieved to alight at the rest-house beside the river. We both felt dirty and tired. Crowds of Dinka were fishing and bathing. My husband, who was talking to Chief Dut, soon found the temptation too much so, ignoring the risk of bilharzia, they both decided to join the bathers. My husband had left his bathing trunks in Tonj so plunged naked into the river before an admiring audience. He turned expecting his companion to follow, only to see Chief Dut putting on a snappy Jansen swimsuit.

During another trek, when twenty miles from Wau, one of the prisoners became very sick. My husband decided that he must be taken without delay to the hospital at Wau. But he himself was busy trying cases in the court, and the driver was unavailable, so he asked me to drive the chap in our three-ton truck. The prisoner was put on a stretcher in the back with some attendants. After about fifteen miles, in the middle of thick bush, I heard a bang on the roof, learned that the prisoner had died, and had to be buried then and there. I refused and, in spite of being told that he would smell before we arrived at Wau, I went on.

Eventually we reached the river Jur. The ghastly ferry had just two narrow wheel tracks which tilted up as the lorry went on and further-more there was nothing to stop the lorry going over the end of the platform into the river. All my passengers (except the corpse) had got off for safety. I found it altogether terrifying but I gingerly drove the lorry on board. The ferryman pulled us across on the wire. When I reached the hospital the doctor was luckily still there. He had the body taken in immediately and laid on his surgery table. Without further ado he took a bottle of snuff and put it under the 'dead' man's nose. The result may have been predictable to him but I found it startling. The prisoner soon found himself under lock and key once more.'

This intrepid wife might have had less anxiety over the ferry had her husband's three-tonner been the smaller Bedford type pick-up which after the war gradually replaced the old lorries. An improvement in many ways, they also had disadvantages, such as much smaller cabs, too sweatily uncomfortable for three adults in that heat. So when on trek

Negotiating a flooded road

91

with his wife the husband had the added tiring chore of driving. The police driver then had to suffer the indignity of sitting at the back with the servants, already overcrowded and perilously perched on impedimenta. The art of loading this smaller, lower-sided pick-up did not come easily to the servants and had at first to be supervised.

'As well as our beds and all our trek furniture, there were the cook boxes and the lamps; then there were all the passengers – our three servants, the driver, the Nuer interpreter and usually two policemen, all of whom of course had their own personal baggage. Once on our way back from Bor we heard bangs on the roof of the cab, the agreed signal to stop. "What is the matter?" my husband asked. A lamp had fallen off. This was repeated two or three times more with different items until my exasperated husband said firmly, "Right, that's the last time I'm stopping. Make sure everything is secure." Not much later there was again frantic banging. "What has fallen off *this* time?" he shouted back angrily. There was no answer, everyone then was convulsed with laughter. Looking out of my window I saw two thin black legs with fluffy white anklets waving about in the ditch. What had fallen off was our wash boy, Tam Lam, very shaken and bruised, but fortunately without broken bones.'

In the dry weather as uncomfortable to traverse as the dried clay 'cotton soil', criss-crossed with cracks, was hard sand that had become cor-

A local bridge

rugated. The lorry shuddered and rattled along, jolting every bone in your body. Much as everyone disliked this hard sand, it did not cause the same concern and apprehension as soft, deep drifting sand. This required an experienced driving skill: with too much acceleration, the wheels would spin deeper and deeper into the sand, as in snow; too little, and there was not enough power to start the lorry moving. In such areas the driver never set off without two sheets of corrugated tin to put under the wheels once they had been dug out. Moving off successfully, he would have to slow down or stop so that the small boy who had retrieved the sheets could jump on. This often meant that the lorry came to an involuntary halt yet again. A mile or two of this soft sand before the railway station at Rahad made catching the train there a perpetual anxiety.

What a difference it would have made to all the members of the Sudan Political Service (and their wives) if only they had been issued with the four-wheel drive 'jeep' or Land Rover. This was being used by the Sudan Defence Force: indeed one was lent to a D.C. and his wife in 1950 when transferred from Nyala to Wau. They were amazed because 'not once did it stick in the sand'. An inherited government policy of 'wise caution' militated against the introduction of anything new, substantiated by the invariable excuse of economy. Lack of money can be frustrating but for the men it sometimes had its compensation: they felt noble and heroic battling against all odds. Some of the women, with less on their minds, couldn't help thinking of practical ways in which, with relatively little expense, conditions might have been improved or comfort increased. But spending money for these reasons was just not considered, so everyone continued to drink water from evil-tasting goatskins, and the battle of the sand continued too. One wife who complained of the lack of a windscreen in 1934, 'because it was so painful when running into clouds of locusts', continued, 'I alternated between feeling deeply depressed and rather splendid. I knew that wives who had come out earlier than I would be scornful of any complaint of mine and say, "Oh, *I* used to do that journey on a camel".'

✳　　✳　　✳

It might be surprising that wives in the nineteen-twenties, straight from constrained drawing rooms, could clamber nonchalantly and unceremoniously on to a camel. But they did. The following description of camel trekking from Khashm el Girba in 1927 confirms this.

'We were away on camel trek for more than half the time each winter. We usually stopped at a head shaikh's village or encampment. I suppose I was the first European woman that most of them had seen. They were all most hospitable though somewhat short of food them-

selves. They gave us camel's milk and a sort of grain drink called
abray. This was often followed by sweet tea in little glasses and then
coffee in small handleless cups sometimes brewed in front of us by a
slave girl. I was surprised to know that many of the more important
shaikhs owned one or more slave girls. They and their parents had
often been with the shaikh's family for generations. They usually
seemed well content, but if they wanted their freedom they could go
to the District Commissioner and demand it, when they were at once
freed. The difficulty was, what would they do thereafter? Prostitu-
tion was the obvious line, but sometimes it was arranged for them to
marry into the Police Force, which worked extremely well. The slave
girls danced on festive occasions: as the tempo increased their top
clothing was slipped off. When the Governor-General came to the
big tribal gathering at Khashm el Girba it was considered unsuitable
for the dance girls to expose so much of themselves and they were
issued with little white B.B.s (bras) – this was not a government
instruction and it produced roars of laughter from the assembled
natives.

When going on trek all belongings had to be the right shape to be
tied onto a camel. We each had a bedding roll which contained camp
beds. We also had a *tisht* (bowl) which was fairly big and had a leather
cover fastened over the top of it. This contained washing requisites
and in my case was my 'vanity box'. Extra or change of clothing were
put into a *girba*, the skin of a sheep or goat sewn to make a tubular
container with an opening at the neck. It had leather loops from the
legs so that it could hang on a camel saddle. In 1927 it was not considered suitable for an English female to wear trousers. I had a drill
skirt which unbuttoned enough to allow me to get on a camel. Once
on, of course, you sat with one leg on each side of the pommel. I
always wore a large felt *terai* because we fussed much more then
about getting sunstroke than we did at a later date. We each had our
own riding camel and the cook had another camel, which also carried
the "cook boxes" and a most important item, the *kanun*. The *kanun*,
a four-legged iron frame, stood over a fire on the ground and every-
ing, including a three-course dinner, was cooked on it. Other camels
carried water, a tent and various necessities, including food for the
camels themselves as we often travelled over apparently barren
sandy or stony ground.

We were woken with tea at 5 a.m. before dawn, and started on trek
at 5.30. It was sometimes quite cold before the sun was up. We usually rode on till 9.30 or 10 a.m. by which time I was ravenous for
breakfast, which often became "brunch" and we didn't have a meal
again till the evening. We stopped during the day in any shade available, or had the tent put up until 3 p.m. and then rode on till dark.

On the whole I enjoyed riding a camel and for long distances it proved less tiring than riding a pony. We didn't go much faster than five or six miles an hour but often travelled up to thirty miles a day. Choosing a stopping place for the night depended on possible grazing or water for the camels, or the necessity to visit some shaikh or village. The country was mostly flat and pretty bare with some thorn bushes in some areas and a covering of grass turned yellow after the rains. Lavatory accommodation was often a problem but when we visited a shaikh's encampment he usually provided the necessary hole in the ground and surrounded it with either a grass shelter or a camel carpet.'

A few years later another camel-riding wife, by now wearing 'loose linen trousers', also recorded that she preferred being perched on top of a camel, where she could benefit from any available breeze, to being cooped up in the hot cab of a lorry.

As much skill was needed in choosing a good camel as in choosing a horse. Those D.C.s habitually trekking by camel became experts. Later on, when motor transport became available, and camels used only occasionally, the D.C.s no longer had their own riding camels but had to hire them. A bad camel provided a terrible ride. In the event of a choice, the best animal would automatically be given by any Muslim to the man in preference to the woman. On one trek in 1943, a wife set off 'fearing the worst' and soon found herself suffering as if from seasickness. She belonged to the generation that did not like to complain, so she didn't. By the end of the trek she could not move and had to be carried into the rest-house and laid on a bed. Her husband could not understand her predicament until he himself tried her camel, when he had to admit that he too found it an appalling ride.

❋   ❋   ❋

Except for the northern part of Sudan, where most preferred camels, D.C's used Arab ponies for trekking during the rains. They were given a forage allowance for two riding horses for their own use and for six to eight pack or 'hamla' ponies for the servants and the baggage. The *syce* liked to have almost as many stable boys as ponies so the total grain bill for the entourage became significant. Great oneupmanship lay in acquiring and owning a 'good' horse, whether for trek alone or for polo. It proved an advantage for a wife to be able to ride and to understand the fairly frequent talk about snaffles and spavin. If they could not ride already they often had lessons before coming out or their husbands patiently taught them when they arrived. A mere novice could enjoy a gentle potter in the cool of the morning before breakfast or in the late afternoon.

'Riding out from Rashad along any odd path, across open country, with no human habitation in sight in any direction, gave an inkling of what the early American settlers may have felt as they set off West into the limitless unknown.'

The more expert wives found riding a good form of exercise and preferable to walking, particularly if this had to be in deep sand, as around El Obeid. They would probably have enjoyed pony trekking if called upon to do so, but this usually occurred in the rains when they were normally not allowed to remain in the district. By an extraordinary oversight on the part of authority, one wife in 1928 actually did remain in a so-called closed district in the Nuba mountains. So she and her husband set out across the plain with a long cavalcade of eight mules.

'When we reached the base of a jebel the young men of the tribe carried all our trek furniture and cooking pots up to the village at the top of the hill. They had settled up here to avoid being taken off as slaves or attacked by other tribes. The women were naked, except that the married ones wore a tuft of leaves fore and aft.'

The ferry at Wau

Some riding camels in Darfur

The police found mules useful mounts in these rocky jebels, being tougher and surer-footed than ponies. Both mules and pack ponies varied greatly in character, intelligence and physique. Curiously neither horses nor mules were ever shod.

＊　　＊　　＊

In certain areas of the south where there was a risk of trypanosomiasis, horses could not be kept, so here there was a certain amount of trekking on foot. This was also a good, if not the only possible, method in parts of the swampy Sudd which stretched either side of the Nile from Malakal to Shambe. One indomitable wife recalls that 'there were often rivers to wade across but if they were too deep I just hung on to my horse's tail and let him do the swimming. I always took two sets of divided skirts and shirts with me. One I wore while the other dried on a stick across the shoulders of my personal porter. I usually wore sneakers but my husband made himself a pair of sandals out of buffalo hide which he found more comfortable and which lasted longer than any other pair of shoes he ever had.' It was not very interesting walking

97

through the 'papyrus' reeds of the Sudd because they were well over six feet high. So it is easy to understand the urge this husband had to try to see above them.

'Once on our way back to the boat after a long and weary day J. climbed a tree to get a bird's eye view of the river. I followed him with our field glasses. I didn't get far, as he had disturbed a nest of red ants. In a second they were swarming all over me, stinging like red hot needles. I screamed and jumped from the tree. The porters tactfully melted away as they knew I should have to remove all my clothes and pick the brutes off one by one.'

Another wife, also trekking in the Sudd during the late 1940s, but stationed at Fangak wrote:

'I always preferred trekking to sitting alone at home. We did occasional trips in the Province paddle-steamer to visit tribal chiefs at court centres on Zeraf island and elsewhere near the river. To more inland places we had to trek on foot. We crossed the Zeraf in a shallow dugout canoe to the island on the other bank. We then set off in a long procession just as seen in funny pictures, the porters ahead each carrying some load, then our servants, then the two of us, followed by a personal bodyguard. On that particular occasion I remember I was wearing a pair of my husband's old football shorts, an Aertex shirt and tennis shoes. In spite of wearing a hat I became very red in the face before we arrived at the one-room rest-house. The servants started to unpack and put up our mosquito-proof room or tent. Because it had been so hot I had never thought of packing a cardigan. We were really cold one evening and had to sit wrapped up in our sheets. I never forgot a cardigan again.

Before we set off on any trek instructions would go ahead to prepare the necessary lavatory. A large hole was dug, then roofed over to leave only a small opening. This would later be surrounded by a *zariba* of reeds. The first time I went on trek with P. we found that two little holes had been made, side by side, in the enclosure: rather a nice idea I thought. Initially we used to take a specially-made wooden box to put over the hole; but we soon didn't bother with this any more and just squatted.'

The Arabs of course always squatted when relieving themselves, a practical recourse in view of the often fierce horizontal desert winds. But European men continued through habit to stand. Perhaps on occasion husbands might have been faintly irritated by the wives' persistent demand for privacy for this natural function. However, after the War at any rate, the husbands took great pains and trouble to organise the necessary provisions.

'On trek we had a canvas bath but no loo. T. had a folding seat made but had the greatest difficulty in explaining to the carpenter exactly what he wanted and why. Once, the villagers had put up the neces-sary semicircular matting, but it was only three foot wide and had been tied to the poles so that it was three feet from the ground. I spent an uncomfortable morning until T. had finished his court case and I could ask him to have the mat lowered. I found it an improve-ment, but not exactly perfect as I then sat looking at the staring villa-gers over the top!'

It was probably this lack of privacy that worried wives most. 'Where-ver we went I appeared to be an object of curiosity and interest. I found this unnerving and sometimes disagreeable. There was so often a crowd of children in attendance and no hope of slipping away and being on my own.' The ever-present flock of children and locals who besieged the visitor resembled crowds in Britain which to this day gather along streets to gaze on passing royalty, motivated partly by curiosity, partly by respect. However, wives in Sudan felt in no way remotely akin to royalty.

Even darkness did not bring protection, as most officials on trek sat outside to eat and read and their bright Petromax lamp acted as an inadvertent and inconvenient spotlight. Scrutiny was inevitable because a government rest-house had to be located near to a major vil-lage.

Trekking with porters, Fangak

After the duck shoot

Over the country, rest-houses varied in comfort from four stars to none. Usually they looked like enlarged editions of the local *tukl* or hut, with either reed or mud walls and a thatched roof. Seasoned wives became inured to snakes, bats or smells which they confronted without a blink, but starry-eyed brides were taken aback.

'On my first trek we stopped at a pleasant-looking thatched shed in a small compound surrounded by a low green hedge, and soon found ourselves shaking hands with the elders drawn up in line to greet us. As our servants started to carry our boxes into the compound, to my amazement first a donkey, then a couple of goats scuttled out of the house followed by several squawking chickens. "Oh dear", I said to my husband in dismay, "where shall we sleep now?" "Why?" he asked, abstractedly. I explained "Well," he replied, shrugging his shoulders and turning back to his chiefs, "they've all gone haven't they?" Which of course they had.'

The upkeep and state of each rest-house was the responsibility of the local chief. Even though used by all the government services and not just the Political, a rest-house would have been occupied for only a few days each month; naturally other uses were found for it in between times. Sometimes there were less obvious but more permanent residents:

'On one trek we came to a rest-house with mud walls (quite a rarity in

100

the South where they are usually grass), with a little window in one wall. I wanted a bath so I shoved my *topi* into the hole. I called our servant and asked him to bring the canvas bath and some warm water. For the first time on trek I felt that I would be sheltered from the eyes of the locals, a privacy difficult to achieve as most of them had never seen a white woman before. Anyway on that one occasion I had a very relaxed and refreshing bath. The next morning when I went to retrieve my *topi* I was amazed to see it moving. At first I thought there might be a snake under it, but when I touched it with a stick, the whole thing fell to pieces. White ants had made a meal of it during the night.'

When a mechanical breakdown late in the day ruled out reaching a rest-house before dark, then a camp site had to be selected. This young A.D.C. presumably left the choice to his servant who sensibly elected to be as near to the source of water as possible to save himself the labour of carrying it too far.

'One night on trek in Darfur we slept without a tent beside a kind of pit. There was an enormous collection of wells and the ground all round them had become turbid and dirty from the herds of cows which came there to drink. Very early next morning our baggage-train moved off to reach our next destination, leaving us marooned on two camp beds, closely surrounded by cattle, horses, shouting people, and goats. We found it a little difficult to get up, dress publicly and, skirting round the interested cows, eat breakfast with governmental dignity.'

Another wife had an equally public awakening some few years later, in 1941.

'We usually slept outside under mosquito nets. One morning my husband had to go off early and I woke to find the village shaikh sitting on the ground beside my bed with a tray of tea. I appreciated the gesture if not the tea and we exchanged courtesies and sustained long silences broken ocasionally by more courtesies. After some time I wondered how to extricate myself. By now a little crowd had gathered and were also seated on the ground. In desperation I called for our servant Daldun. He told the shaikh that the sun was now hot and it was time the lady went in to dress. The old man rose and took his leave. The crowd were less easy to move and Daldun had to come back again to shoo them away from peering into the hut before I could finally start to dress.'

A husband as well as a wife could be embarrassed by the Arab custom of presenting a live sacrifice to any visiting traveller: on his part, because he often knew the gift could ill be spared by the donor; on hers, because the victim would usually be despatched within sight and sound. 'Goats and sheep were slain in traditional hospitality but once a poor

wretched goat was tied up outside our hut, bleating all night. Its liver and kidneys were served up fresh for us at breakfast.' Apart from this disadvantage, gifts of food were easier to accept as they proved a great benefit to the servants who, for once, would be able to enjoy a really good meal. Sometimes the hospitable gift seemed almost too lavish:
'Once when we arrived at a cattle camp the usual great gourds of fro-thing milk were brought, but this time there remained too much even for all the servants. I decided to have our trek bath filled with the surplus milk and then sat in it like Cleopatra. My skin, dried by a whirling sandstorm earlier in the day, really did begin to feel soft again. But I have an uncomfortable thought that next day we proba-bly both smelt rather cheesy.'
However generous the hospitality, no meat could last longer than two days in that heat and so husbands always took guns on trek, to feed servants as well as masters. Just as some wives learned to ride when they came out, so also some learned to shoot.
'My husband had been teaching me how to shoot with a twelve-bore, so suggested I had a try at a flock of duck near a lake. I crawled up the bank and suddenly saw so very many duck that in my excitement, and oblivious of all my training, I shot quickly from the hip, nearly knocking myself over. To my utter amazement I found I had shot eleven duck with one cartridge. I then had a great reputation as a shot because, as the Nuer continued to relate, the D.C. could shoot only one duck at a time when in the air and very often not even that.'
Another wife was offered a shot at a crocodile in Blue Nile Pro-vince.
'When visiting Roseires I was asked whether I would like to shoot a crocodile. I was told to stalk very quietly, keep hidden behind a rock until close enough to peep over and then I should be ready to shoot very quickly. I duly followed all the instructions. When I popped my head over the top I looked straight into a crocodile's face only a yard or so away. I am afraid that both he and I reacted so violently to seeing each other that no shot was fired and he disappeared into the water with fantastic rapidity.'
As this venture was pure sport no-one felt dismayed by lack of suc-cess, but if the quarry was the ubiquitous guinea fowl, its dry white flesh so useful for the pot, then it became a matter of importance to all con-cerned: 'We saw a huge flock of guinea fowl on the ground but, after bumping up and down all day in the lorry, my hand was none too steady. I also knew I should never be able to look the servants in the face if I missed and that made it unsteadier still. Luckily for my honour, I hit three before they flew away.'
At the same time, just after the War, one couple in the south used to go out most evenings for a walk with their guns in an effort to supple-

ment the meat ration:

'One evening, while walking in the forest accompanied by two stalwart Dinka, we went for a long time without seeing anything. Then at last we came upon some water-buck and crept up behind a tree to try to have a shot at them. I thought I heard shouts of *asad* (lion) and we turned to see our escort running away. J. quickly loaded his rifle and peered into the bushes. I loaded my .22 although I knew it wouldn't be much use. I thought I actually saw a lion in some grass

Shoebill stork (Balaeniceps rex)

about thirty yards away. My heart leapt with excitement. I was mentally preparing for death when I saw to my horror that J. was running after the others. I called frantically, "It's a lion. Come and shoot it." He shouted back, "No, it's bees. Run." Our guides had said *asl* (honey). No amount of running could help me now. The bees were all around me. They were in my hair, down my neck, everywhere, and I was being stung all over.'

As well as trying their hand at shooting, some wives became interested in, and tried to identify, the many exotic and unusual birds. 'I had learned about the unique *Balaeniceps rex* as a theoretical example when I was at Oxford. I can still remember my excited surprise when on trek once, south of Talodi, in the early rains, I suddenly and unexpectedly saw a whole cohort of those odd Shoe-Bill Storks stomping round a flooded *hufar*. (I have a private theory that the stuffed specimen in the Pitts-River Museum was the prototype for Lewis Carroll's Dodo.)'

No ornithological knowledge was needed to recognise other larger birds, such as the nonchalant apathetic ostrich, the neat town-spinster of a demoiselle crane, or the lumbering ground hornbill, whose huge black wings could hardly lift it into the air. For some reason this bird was considered unlucky in parts of Kordofan and would cause shrieks of apprehension when sighted. Apart from this the locals showed little interest in birds unless useful for the pot. 'When an unusual bird with a blue flash swept past the cab as we were driving we would call back. "What was that?" The prosaic and dismissive reply was often the same. "It was a bird – just a bird", as if we had supposed it be a djinn or flying saucer. They were not much more helpful over the names of trees.'

Many wives were intrigued by, and sketched, flowers, shrubs or trees but unfortunately the majority of these came into flower and leaf during the rains. In many a place in the Sudan there would have been more vegetation had it not been for the ubiquitous and esurient goat. These creatures gobbled up every emerging seedling and all too effectively prevented any natural regeneration, which could be proved by simply enclosing an area with goat-proof fencing; in due time this would become a green shrubbery amid the surrounding barren sand. A more sudden transformation was effected by the first rain, when overnight patches of bright green would miraculously appear and exotic bulbs burst forth.

As breathtakingly beautiful to any foreigner were the spectacular sunsets; what a challenge they would have been to Turner or the Impressionists. The Sudanese, unlike the Chinese, appeared to take little aesthetic pleasure in nature and ignored the sublime; Arabs in particular preferred the enclosed, the miniature and neat geometrical patterns. They rarely commented on another marvel that followed the sunsets, when the whole vast 'floor of heaven' was indeed 'thick inlaid with patines of bright gold'. (Though as one wife commented it should have been 'silver' except that that was one syllable too long.)

In general the wives wrote at greater length about trekking than about any other aspect of their life in the country. Evidently they had enjoyed seeing more of the country and more of its people. Enthusiastically as they may have set out on trek, towards the end when food, reading matter and clean clothes began to run out, when tolerance of dust and heat began to wane, they might have echoed an honest comment that, 'One of the joys of trekking was the thrill of arriving home again and being able to relax in a comfortable chair, have the first iced drink for days and sleep once more on a proper bed.' This wife might also have added that an additional reward would be to find accumulated mail from the U.K.

＊

11 *Sitting with Sitts*

Talking to the local ladies (*sitts*) was generally only possible in those parts of Sudan where Arabic was spoken. However some wives made successful attempts to communicate with the Nuba. 'I was meant to chat up the village women while B. was in court. The Nuba didn't speak Arabic so we had to manage with sign language, which caused shrieks of laughter all round.' Another wife, also there just before the War, came prepared. 'When we were in England my husband had brought a collection of toy animals. I used to take these to the women's quarters and spread them out for everyone to see. Then they would tell me their names in their own local language. I found this invaluable for breaking through the shyness and establishing some communication between us. They realised that they would appear strange to us just as we did to them. Once I remember them screaming with laughter when they showed the little wooden head-rests they used at night to protect their elaborate coiffures, which were in fact very similar to the blocks used for the same purpose by European ladies in the eighteenth century.'

In the northern Sudan, the prevalent strict *purdah* and the resulting shyness proved more of a barrier than the lack of a communicating language. Most British wives, except perhaps at the very start of their first tour, learned enough Arabic to cope with the limited topics of conversation. To encourage them to improve their Arabic, the Government introduced around 1929 a special Arabic exam for wives, and two of the contributors wrote about preparing for it and then passing it. During the War this exam was dropped, accounting for the fact that another wife took and passed in 1946 the Probationer's stiffer qualifying Higher Arabic exam. Exactly how wives opted to learn the language varied with circumstances; one spent a year at Manchester University

106

before coming out in 1926, a second, after her arrival in El Obeid, paid for lessons from the local headmistress, and a third took advantage of a boringly long journey out by sea.

'When I travelled out as a bride in 1945 the ship had to go slowly and circuitously in convoy, consequently it took a tedious three weeks to reach Alexandria. To pass the time my husband taught me the basic elements of Arabic as we sat on our life-jackets around the deck (the ship was carrying twice the normal number of passengers so there were never enough chairs under cover.) I was grateful for this start ever afterwards, as it meant that I could look up any word I wanted in Hillelson's *Sudan Arabic* on my own; and in later years I attempted to manage a Girl Guide company in Omdurman, and became eligible for a temporary job in the Sudan Pilot Population project.'

Time and opportunity to meet local ladies arose on trek. Not all wives found it easy to chat nonchalantly and casually. Some, particularly in the early years who had no precedent to follow, felt inhibited by an anxiety over local custom and practice. A wife who arrived in Kassala Province in 1932 wrote:

'I was terrified when my husband suggested that I should visit the women. I had very little self-confidence and even less Arabic. A year or two later I did become captivated by the friendliness and charm of these nomadic women. By then I could produce the photo of my baby (left at home in England with my mother) and found another topic of conversation to be my 'bun'. They often asked me to unpin it to prove that I had quite long hair, as theirs never grew to any length.'

Nomadic tribes, less constrained by *purdah,* proved more forthcoming, as this particular wife also found when she came out in 1926. Having learned some Arabic at home and not by nature shy, she conversed on a wider range of subjects:

'I remember the women being so sorry for me. Had I no mother? No sisters? Was I on my own? Not even pregnant? Why was I treated like a piece of luggage going around with my husband? Why had I not been left at home? It seemed all very odd and very bad to them. One girl, braver than her elders, even asked why the 'Turks' (the whites) smelled like death? On another occasion they wanted to know why we had such bad manners, referring to our habit of saying 'good morning' and then quickly going on with the business in hand, instead of having the courtesy to exchange endless comments on the weather, crops and families.'

It was a strict code of Muslim hospitality that drinks and food should always be produced for any traveller or visitor. Even those who could ill afford it offered lavish provisions, producing 'various kinds of sweet drinks or very sweet tea or equally sweet Turkish coffee.' Sugar being expensive, and refreshments taking time to prepare, it was sad that the results turned out to be the very antithesis of thirst-quenching. In that dry heat the greatest luxury would have been a glass of clear, ice-cold, tasteless water. Courtesy demanded that anything proffered should at least be sampled and if possible nearly finished. Subterfuges had to be used to avoid hurt feelings; when being entertained outside, porous sand could be used to advantage. Nearly everyone enjoyed the local coffee though, despite its excessive sweetness:

'It took several hands to make the coffee. One woman pounded the beans with a pestle in a mortar, another fanned the charcoal, a third brought the little round earthenware coffee pot. With the coffee inside, it was placed at a tilt on a bead ring, then another woman pushed a wisp of grass down the straight neck to act as a filter. This delicious strong black coffee was the best that ever came my way. Curiously I had never liked coffee before going to the Sudan.'

Customary Arab generosity in another realm meant that visitors had to be careful about complimentary remarks. The unwary could find themselves presented with the possession in question:

'On one trek we stopped at an Arab encampment and, while the men carried on their business, I called on the ladies. As usual I found their

D.C.'s wife with Girl Guide company in her garden in Omdurman, 1951

108

welcome friendly and generous. Soon a crowd had gathered to see the curious stranger while we enjoyed the usual drinks. In an unguarded moment I asked about some scent which I think they said was derived from honey. Sudanese ladies are very fond of strong scent. Just as I was about to leave my hostess came forward and emptied a bottle of scent over me. When I rejoined the men they, less than gallant, said they found the smell overpowering. Only time and much washing managed to remove the pungent smell.'

Most of these visits never progressed beyond the initial almost ceremonial introduction. Made on trek, they might not be repeated owing to transfers. One wife who remained in the Sudan throughout the war built up more of a relationship.

'In Singa I came to know quite well the complicated 'family' of Mek Hassan, who visited me in return and gradually became more forthcoming. Surprised that I was the only wife, they thought I must be very lonely. (Muslims could, and sometimes did, have four wives simultaneously). The women thought it must be very distressing for me living so far away from my mother, "for did not one love one's mother more than one's husband?" Of course they were *really* sorry for me because at that time we had no children. Had I no relation who would have a child for me? One of the ladies had actually done this for one of her relations and offered to do it for me!'

An effort to start a more permanent connection in the years before the War was doomed to failure because the wives stayed out for such a comparatively short time. 'We stayed on trek almost three weeks out of four in Gedaref but while in the station I held a dressmaking class for the wives of the *Markaz* (office) staff, helping them to master the intricacies of Singer sewing machines which, by 1938, had made their way into most towns and some villages. Unfortunately all too soon I had to return to England.' A similar venture in another province also came to an abrupt end when a wife tried to teach some older girls embroidery stitches. 'We had hardly achieved anything before the time came to go on leave.' Another wife progressed from spinning cotton to teaching the women to knit. 'We made squares which later could be sewn together to make a cover. It gave them pleasure and a new interest, but after I left I doubt whether there was ever a finished result.'

After the War, when Sudanese entered the Political Service, an opportunity arose for wives in the same station to meet. With the best intentions, the gap between the two cultures seemed too wide to bridge.

'Through our husbands I invited the wife of the first Sudanese A.D.C. in Rashad to come to visit me from next door. It took several weeks to achieve this visit and in the end I'm afraid she was probably 'ordered' to come. She set off with her mother-in-law, even more amply built than she herself, who had to sit on a stool every few paces, which a servant picked up and put down each time. Progress was very slow but eventually they arrived. Both remained muffled up with only their eyes showing because of the presence of our servant who brought in first the lemonade and then the tea. We went through the names and ages of her children and then the names and ages of ours. She volunteered nothing and I found it difficult to think of anything else to say.'

One of the reasons why the elderly mother-in-law could walk only a few steps might have been the uncomfortable aftermath of several births following female 'circumcision'. How the Arab women ever produced any children is difficult for a European to imagine. The universal and barbaric practice of genital mutilation, whether infibulation or clitoridectomy, would make intercourse painful. There could be no birth without preliminary slashing and subsequent cobbling together by, in the majority of cases, untrained locals using septic tools. The courageous efforts of one Governor-General's wife immediately after the War, and the constant teaching and preaching of the Midwives' Training School, did nothing to alter public opinion. The custom continues to this day. According to the magazine *Sudanow* (December 1984) there are still eighty-four million women in thirty countries suffering recurring and unnecessary pain. The apparent determination of Arab women, enduring this primitive treatment, to continue to inflict it on the next generation, is shocking. All efforts of educated Sudanese women, would-be reformers, have so far had little effect, partly because they are so few in number. Only in 1946 was the first girl accepted at Khartoum University. In the nineteen-forties and 'fifties the wives of Sudanese officials would have had, at the most, elementary education. Many would not be allowed to eat in their husband's presence. It took a long time for the European way of life to affect local customs and traditions; even then, only those few who had benefited from higher education were likely to be influenced. Some exceptions proved the rule and in these cases both sides appeared to benefit.

'In Nyala in the early 'fifties we lived next to the Sudanese A.D.C., and his wife, Zeinab, became a great friend of mine. I saw her almost daily when we were not on trek. My husband never saw her at all because she had to be in *purdah*. She taught me how to make my own flour, since all the time I was in the country we had to make our own bread; without yeast, we had to use native beer. She also showed me how to cook several delicious Sudanese dishes which we still enjoy from time to time. One winter morning over coffee she told me of her latest epoch-making discovery. "Now that we need a blanket at night I have discovered that it is far more comfortable and less prickly to put another sheet on top of the bed."

She had the usual very elaborate hair-do which took four days to

A market north of Atbara

complete. Hundreds of tiny partings were made and every hair woven into a plait. Because their hair will not grow long, Sudanese women weave in pieces of silk and plait the hair until it reaches waist level. They considered it unclean to have any hair except on their heads, so they removed it elsewhere by making a paste of lemon juice and sugar, letting it harden and then pulling it off sharply. Subjected to this treatment on my legs, I didn't like it at all!'

Even this promising relationship soon ended because of the inevitable transfer of one of the pair. More hope of continuity existed in Khartoum where certain members of the S.P.S. moved into specialist branches and hence became less liable to transfer.

'In 1944, my husband being Assistant Civil Secretary – Prisons, I had contact with some most entertaining women: the long-sentence murderesses in Khartoum North prison. I taught them knitting which they loved but we had to give it up for lack of materials. I started them on patchwork which was a great success. There must be some of our counterpanes still in existence as they were in great demand by the European community.

111

When the time came for us to leave the Sudan I minded leaving those women very much. We had become very friendly and they were occasionally allowed to come to tea with me. My final farewell to them in the prison became a very weepy occasion. The wardress wept, I wept and the eight prisoners all wept too. I think, now, I should have a place in the *Guinness Book of Records* as the only person to have been kissed by eight murderesses in one afternoon.'

Continuity could be achieved through clubs and associations in Khartoum and province headquarters, where there were other government officials' wives as well as the Political's. In Khartoum a Sudan Women's Association was founded in 1944 for which all women who could speak and understand English became eligible. A Governor's wife started a similar club in Kassala in 1950.

'I was involved in starting a Ladies' Club on the lines of the Women's Institute. The Province Education Officer gave us coaching on the mornings of the meetings so that we could say the essentials of what we wanted to explain to the members in an understandable way, since the Arabic that women used differed from that used by men. The compound of the Girls' School made an obvious meeting-place as it had a ten-foot high wall all around it. The Sudanese wives who were not allowed to be seen out in daylight could make their way there at dusk. A police guard was provided to ensure privacy; but as these men used to sit on top of the wall and take a great interest in all

A girls' school in a village near Wadi Halfa

112

the proceedings, the object of their presence seemed partly defeated.

Many members said they wanted to learn how to read and write, so before the main meeting began we had half an hour's class given by the local teachers. Our programme included toy-making, home first-aid, and cookery demonstrations of favourite dishes from different countries, as our membership included seven nationalities. Making paper flowers proved particularly popular, but it caused the only discord. Two ladies decided they must have the same roll of crêpe paper and proceeded to wage a tug-of-war accompanied by high piercing shrieks. Fortunately another roll of the same coloured paper appeared, and everyone settled down happily once more.

Against all odds the meetings succeeded, muddles and misunderstandings being sorted out with goodwill and laughter. Perhaps our greatest achievement lay in the fact that we were all in it together and determined to have a good time.'

In Khartoum children of different nationalities met in various play-schools and older girls at the Unity High School, 'established in 1928 by the Church Missionary Society to provide a Christian English type of secondary education for those who desire it'. (*Educational Development in the Sudan 1898-1956*, by Mohammed Omer Beshir, 1969). A wife who spent her last ten years in Khartoum came to know some of the girls at this school very well indeed.

'When I started to teach at the Unity High School in about 1948 I made a host of friends among the parents. The newly-appointed headmistress felt determined that some of her girls should be among the first qualified doctors. At that time the entrance to the Kitchener School of Medicine required a credit in maths; but only arithmetic was taught at the school. I had a maths degree, so agreed to take the Certificate form straight away, and the top three forms the following year. Four girls made up this Certificate form; one Greek, one Armenian, one Egyptian and one real Sudanese, who was a darling and I became very fond of her. She lived with her uncle who happened to by my husband's assistant. All four of the girls passed, one with distinction.'

Education of both sexes remained a problem in the Sudan because of the completely different Roman and Arabic scripts, quite apart from all the innumerable indigenous languages. Pitifully few Sudanese parents allowed their daughters to be educated beyond the age of eleven, if they were allowed to be educated at all. As the Sudan Graduates Conference reported in 1942,'Girls' education is so backward that it cannot be compared with any other country . . . the country's progress is to a great extent retarded by the ignorance of the Sudanese women.' At that time the Sudanese men could be forgiven for making the main aim of girls' education 'the production of suitable wives and mothers' rather than the intellectual fulfilment of the girls themselves.

Since 1921 a few girls had been trained annually at pre-secondary level to become teachers but, because of the early marriage age, they did not teach for long. Other girls and older women had the courage to attend the Midwives' Training School in Omdurman, and felt no anxiety at being in mixed company. One midwife joined a couple on trek in Darfur during the 'forties. 'These midwives had a tough time trying to put over their new ideas, even those of basic hygiene. They were women of character and I admired Sitt Sowa very much. She went out with such staunchness to face the antagonistic traditionalism of her countrywomen.'

These brave Sudanese midwives and teachers were consequently more emancipated than the wives of notables, Ministers, or Members of Parliament at the time of self-determination. An S.P.S. wife in Omdurman from 1949–52 always found herself the only woman at all the innumerable tea and dinner parties she attended there. She wrote, 'only once did we manage to persuade two young Sudanese officials to bring their wives with them when they came to tea with us. Alas, it was not a success. The charming girls, wrapped in their white *thawbs*, were very shy, ate practically nothing and hardly spoke, even when coaxed by their husbands.'

Each nationality, including the British, had its own club in Khartoum. They tended to keep to themselves for their own leisure pursuits, apart that is from a few individual friendships. Some years before Independence a new racecourse was opened together with an International Club. This did not lead to a new burst of international socialising. Perhaps not many women were interested in racing or perhaps each secretly thought that, to misquote Ogden Nash,

> *'Their own kin and kith*
> *Were more fun to be with.'*

✳

114

12 *Coping with Children*

Rarely did members of the Political Service possess their own house in the U.K. when they were first married. If there were no children, leaves were spent either travelling in other countries or between the two sets of parents at home. Before the War such parents usually had servants. The accepted practice was to employ a nanny on the birth of a baby. In the nineteen-twenties a nanny cost only about forty pounds a year, hardly an extravagance even on the A.D.C.'s starting salary of four hundred and eighty pounds per annum. In that stratum of society at that time it was glibly accepted that the nanny would see more of, and do more for, the infant than the mother. This accounts for the apparently nonchalant way in which early wives wrote that they 'left the baby at home with nanny and my mother and went out to join my husband for the winter.' The 'winter' was a matter of three or four months; then during the summer the family would be reunited when the husband came home for his three months' leave.

The following two excerpts give an idea of the type of family arrangements made by women who married in the nineteen-twenties. 'Our three children, all born in my parents' vicarage in Northumberland, were in the care of a nursery-trained nanny, who cost us £1.00 a week. There they remained throughout their school life, apart from one visit to the Sudan in 1937, when my husband first lived in a station (Wad Medani) where children were allowed. The two girls were then nine and seven and a half and our son was eighteen months old.'

The second wife was not in a province headquarters when she brought her children out for the first time, so would not have had the advantage of electricity.

'I left the children with an unflappable Scots nanny and they stayed with their grannies alternately. When James was six and Caroline three I brought them and nanny out to the Sudan for the first time. On reaching Khartoum, Caroline suffered very bad prickly heat. We travelled by train on to El Obeid, where we were lent a car for the next one hundred and fifty miles to Nahud (Kordofan Province).

To accommodate us all my husband had to have a mud-walled room built against the compound wall by some prisoners. This cost us ten pounds for the wood for the roof, doors and windows. Somehow we all managed to share the one tiny bathroom in the house for five months.

We did not have the children out again until we were posted to Dueim, three years later.'

Those wives' decisions may seem surprising to parents today, but at the time they ranged with the consensus of opinion. A wife's duty to her husband took priority over her responsibility to their children. (Even after 1945, a wife about to be married and go out to the Sudan was advised seriously and emphatically by her employer, a woman, 'If it ever comes to a choice between your husband and your children, always put your husband first.')

Another influencing factor must be considered. 'Before the War almost the whole of the Sudan was considered death-dealing to British children', especially certain stations in the south because of their inaccessibility.

'In Raga (later Equatoria Province) in 1931 we had no telephone and no refrigerator; nor a doctor, so of course children were out of the question. Anyway at the first hint of pregnancy the poor wife would have been sent home. Two years later we were transferred to Kajokaji (on the southern border) almost as far from civilisation as Raga, though we did have a missionary couple living nearby, whose first child had died of cerebral malaria. I did not feel at all well and was dogged by bouts of an unidentified fever. When D.C. Yei went on leave we took over his house.

I began to feel better and started the longed-for baby, though I did not quite know how I was going to manage it all.

A few months later I set off for home and caught the Nile steamer at Juba. I knew very little about the details of production so ignored the slight signs of impending miscarriage. On the boat I had no-one to consult except the Engineer and eventually I felt forced to confide in him. He couldn't believe I was having a miscarriage because I looked so healthy. I begged him to alert a doctor in Malakal, a scheduled night stop. Luckily for me a Syrian doctor and a D.C.'s wife, who had been a V.A.D. in World War I, came on board there. They were very kind and attentive, and every night gave me an injection of morphia; during the day they kept me rigorously in bed (the cabin was claustrophobically stuffy) and insisted that I had only cold food.

When we eventually reached Khartoum, two days late, I was taken off to hospital in an ambulance. A few nights later I lost the baby and felt very low and miserable, a mood exacerbated by another bout of dysentery which I had contracted in the hospital.'

It is unlikely that any mother with today's advantages could begin to imagine the utter ignorance of pregnancy and childbirth of that generation of women. Nor did anyone realise at that stage that some unknown factor in the Sudan greatly increased the chance of a miscarriage. The doctors in Government service had little experience of women. In this same year, 1934, the doctor in Fasher 'issued a stern warning in a memorandum: "Wives are *not* to become pregnant in Darfur".' This hopeful edict had been prompted by three simultaneous but coincidental events.

That winter the doctor had been busy dealing with an outbreak of cerebrospinal meningitis so bad that in one village forty out of forty-four children had died. While coping with this he received a telegram that a wife had fallen ill in Nyala.

'The charming and splendid doctor drove the hundred miles to

Playing by the Nile

117

Nyala, took a blood slide from me, played a game of polo, and drove back to Fasher. He then had to drive another hundred miles out west to yet another wife. He took a blood slide and returned. Somehow the slides were muddled up, because sometime later when I was out riding a telegram arrived, "You have tertian malaria: treat accordingly". I presume the other wife was told "Stop making a fuss and get up." In fact, later on we both complicated his responsibilities further by becoming pregnant.

Unfortunately, just as we were about to go home on leave, I was in danger of having a miscarriage. The doctor endeavoured to save me the four days' bumpy drive in a lorry. With considerable difficulty he arranged that I should be given a lift to El Obeid in the plane of the Governor-General, then touring Darfur Province. This aeroplane could take twenty-two passengers and the only British staff with him were the Private Secretary and his A.D.C. My husband, being still on duty and not being ill, did not obtain permission to travel in the plane and had to plough off on the usual four-day lorry trip. It would be difficult to describe my panic at finding myself inside this highly official aeroplane, in considerable pain and in purely male company. All three men seemed at the time stiff and remote beyond words, extremely nice as I later found them to be. They said an embarrassed "Good morning" and ended our communications.

We flew over my husband, a tiny black object creeping over an immense plain, with nothing else moving from one horizon to the other. At El Obeid I parted from the royal anti-miscarriage company as much, I imagine, to their relief as to mine.'

This wife achieved the rest of the journey home without mishap, giving birth to her son the following October. The wife who actually had a miscarriage after her trip on the Nile steamer felt more anxious than ever to start a family so decided to spend the whole of the ensuing year at home 'in order to give the baby from the start the advantage of the English climate and English doctors.' The plan succeeded but meant that the husband had to be left on his own in the Sudan for one complete tour.

Although, before 1939, the majority of Political Service wives returned home – or were officially sent home – to have their babies, one of them succeeded in having her baby in Khartoum during the winter of 1934, an example soon followed by another wife. 'While in Khartoum North in 1934 we visited Shaikh Tayib. He blessed the milk I was given to drink and pronounced that within a year I would bring forth. At the time we had no such intention but in fact Belinda was born in December 1935. At three weeks old she was with us on the Khartoum North's ketch on which my husband habitually spent January to March inspecting his district.'

During the War it became commonplace for babies to be born in Khartoum hospital. 'When I was expecting our second child I travelled to Khartoum a fortnight before it was due. In those days we stayed in hospital for a fortnight after the birth. That meant that friends had to look after our other child for a month. All through the War we became like one big family doing the things for each other that parents and grand-parents would have done had we been in England. We did not always have the chance to repay the person who had helped us, so we just repaid the kindness by helping someone else.'

Sudan had no equivalent to the Indian *ayah* because the better-class girls remained in *purdah*. 'We built a large playpen in the garden under the trees. We knew the garden itself could never be totally safe; snakes could lurk in the grass, scorpions hide in toy boxes and rabid dogs could run in from the street. So when I could not be with the children I always asked a servant to stay on guard and keep an eye on them.' The Sudanese in general, not excepting the servants, value and love children and spoil their own unashamedly. They must have thought our pale, fair-haired little creatures odd, but they never missed an opportunity of playing with them, nor did the guaranteed prisoners, often deputed to be an official's gardener. 'Our gardener used to play happily with our small daughter in the sand pit even though I knew he had been jailed for murder and rape!'

Feeding the children during the War proved far from easy as no one could obtain certain 'necessities', and the choice of food became more limited than in rationed England.

'Baby foods were a problem. We could find no cereals of any kind. The only flour was made from local *dura* and the resulting bread not suitable for small children. When trying to wean them, we had to mash vegetables and make tough meat edible. Once one of our children fell really ill and the doctor said he should have nothing but white rusks. This was impossible. So he put me in touch with an officer in the U.S. Air Force in Omdurman who took me to a hangar stacked from floor to ceiling with cornflakes, tins of all sorts and innumerable bins of white bread. I had not seen any of these things for years.'

After the War a mother had difficulty feeding her daughter for another reason.

'During our second year in Port Sudan I began to be worried by our daughter's intake of food. She looked well fed but would only peck at the food we put before her. Every day the cook and I would make out the daily shopping list and he would solemnly try to think of something that would stimulate her appetite. All to no avail. One day, for some reason, I went to the servant's quarters. They were in the middle of their mid-day meal, squatting round a large dish of

Playing by the Nile

food. There, among their children, was Jennifer, tucking in happily. No wonder she had no appetite for our lunch served an hour later! She and the cook's daughter had become great friends and as a result her Arabic was fluent.'

Being such good mimics at that early age, all the children tended to talk Arabic with a better accent than their mothers.

After 1945, although some people brought out nannies, the majority of women looked after their own children, partly owing to changing attitudes but also for reasons of economy. Salaries had not kept up with inflation and it had become difficult by then to manage without private means. Mothers now voluntarily chose to have their babies in Khartoum Hospital instead of going home, provided that the expected date fell during the winter months. There was known to be a slight risk for the baby whose sweat glands do not start to operate immediately, but this was likely to be serious only in the very high temperatures of the summer. In spite of this drawback one couple had, in 1946, arranged to have their baby born in Khartoum in July.

'The Governor-General had kindly lent us his rest-house in Erkowit and my sister had come out to look after the other children while I went down to Khartoum for the confinement. Richard thought otherwise. He arrived three weeks early, by the light of the cook's torch (the lights in Erkowit were always turned off at eleven o'clock).

Fortunately another wife with nursing experience was staying in the rest-camp at the time.'

Two years later, in 1948, the well-laid plans of another couple went wrong for a different reason.

'Just before I was due to leave Rashad to board the train at Rahad for Khartoum the rail strike began, so my husband had to drive me all the way into El Obeid. It should have been possible to book a flight on the small plane that left Fasher once or twice a week; but all passages for several weeks ahead had already been booked. Luckily the efficient sister cheerfully agreed to look after me in the hospital. Unfortunately a week later several cases of smallpox occurred and she did not consider the hospital safe. So our son was not only the first British baby to be born in El Obeid but the first to be born in a governor's house.'

That wife could be considered lucky. The following year another family only narrowly missed a harrowing disaster twice over. During pregnancy the wife fell so sick for four days that she had to be flown to Khartoum. Eventually she recovered and in due course bore a daughter safely in El Obeid Hospital; but a further crisis arose, the baby nearly died and an emergency christening had to be held.

Although young children could withstand the extreme heat of the country, they certainly did not keep well all the time. Each one gave its parents, at one time or another, many hours if not days of terrifying anxiety. Children succumbed to innumerable infections with frightening suddenness. In a matter of hours their temperatures soared to what in England would be considered danger point. Fortunately penicillin and other drugs developed during the War proved a quick and welcome panacea, their availability enabling and encouraging women with young children to spend all the available months between leaves with their husband in Sudan.

Even so the old pattern of family separation began as soon as the eldest child neared the age of eight and, for both health and educational reasons, had to return to the U.K. 'I was shattered after leaving our eldest son at a prep school; never had an eight-year-old looked so vulnerable nor a red school cap so large. After shutting up the house I travelled back with our sadly depleted family to rejoin my husband.' By the 'forties fewer and fewer grandparents had either house or staff large enough to offer a long-term haven, so most families coping with school holidays had to embark on buying or renting a house in the U.K. The upkeep of this second home together with the boarding school fees meant additional financial worries and difficulties.

During the last few years of the condominium the Government allowed school children to use their allotted annual passage to travel out and back simply for the holidays; consequently family separations for those lucky parents stationed in or near Khartoum became shorter.

'We had to dip into our savings for an air fare for Hugo to come out to see us for the Christmas holidays. But after that the Sudanese had more of a say in Government policy and insisted (bless them) that officials could not be efficient if divided from their families. So children at school in England came out on the official 'Operation Santa'. The last year before we left, all three of ours flew out. I generally managed to be home for their Easter and Summer holidays.'

Inspite of this late concession, one wife worked out that although she had been in the country over a period of twenty-seven years, she had spent only eighty-four months there with her husband. Another calculated that, in the fifteen years of their married life in the Sudan, they had actually been together for only half that time. It is a verifiable fact that despite, or because of, the separations, there were very few divorces in the Service. As one wife summarised, 'the separations from husband and children were awful, but the reunions wonderful.'

❋

13 Khartoum – Home from Home

A wife arriving in Khartoum for the first time in the nineteen-twenties would have been astonished to find the capital 'city' less sophisticated than her own tiny market town back in England. A few tarmac roads existed but the rest were dust. Some splendid buildings stood along the river front; the Palace, the Secretariat, and after a few senior official's houses, the Grand Hotel, built by an English company in return for mining rights. Slightly set back was the Cathedral, still without its tower up to 1931. In the expatriate shopping area were a few one-storeyed, glass-fronted shops, but the majority remained small doorless, windowless cells, invariably spreading their wares across the pavement – or where a pavement would have been, had there been one.

The reason for this was that the Khalifa, who had lived and kept his headquarters in Omdurman, had in the second year of his power razed the then existing Khartoum to the ground. When Sir Herbert (later Lord) Kitchener arrived there in 1898 he found only 'a heap of mud ruins.' As C.E.J.Walkley described in *Sudan Notes and Records* (vol.19) the new town was laid out on a series of Union Jacks, Kitchener placing a gun post in the centre of each 'flag' for purposes of defence. The diagonal roads soon disappeared.

A wife arriving in Khartoum in 1945 expressed as much surprise as her counterpart in the 'twenties. Khartoum reminded her 'of a town in a wild West film'. In the intervening years there had never been enough money for what these wives (and other Western visitors) eccentrically considered urban 'essentials' – such as adequate street lighting and water-borne sewage. For some unknown, or perhaps the same, reason houses in the residential area had neither names nor clear num-

A modern bungalow

bers. One knew each house by its last (or most notorious, or popular) resident as 'So and so's house'. The oldest houses ran west from the Palace along the river bank and behind them stood some spacious bungalows with fine gardens. As the expatriate population increased and the airport developed, new two-storey houses and bungalows sprang up, usually in closer rows and with much smaller gardens. Some wives, prepared to live in towns or suburbia at home, seemed to prefer the unlimited space and peace of out-stations when in Sudan. Not one of the fifteen contributors, who had spent a varying number of years in Khartoum, chose to write at any length about her time there. Despite the luxury of electric light – however dim – and despite the amazing miracle of unlimited water actually running out of a tap, their life in out-stations remained more memorable and vivid.

It is understandable that before the War the less gregarious types would not be pleased to be confronted with the social rules and conventions from which they had just escaped at home. Society then in Khartoum had been stratified officially and subject to protocol. The majority accepted this as they accepted the decisive and divisive distinction between the two British clubs. Any official arriving in Khartoum had to 'sign the book' at the Palace and also to call, or drop cards, on the three senior secretaries, Civil, Legal, and Financial and also to call in on the Commander-in-Chief. This practice, eminently sensible in those early

The garden of one of the original river front houses in Khartoum

The Palace, Khartoum

days, enabled a newcomer to be introduced quickly to general society. After the War the system gradually became more of a formality partly because one could circulate information by telephone; even so, boxes remained on verandas expressly for calling cards.

With or without the extra hospitality which this practice entailed, senior wives in Khartoum found that life for them meant almost non-stop official entertaining, enjoyed or endured according to temperament, and also according to individual financial means, because the official entertainment allowance for a Governor in 1954 totalled a derisory £10 a month.

Younger couples without any of these official obligations could also find it difficult to live on their salary in Khartoum, with a cost of living higher than elsewhere in the country. For some this factor could counterbalance the advantages of having a school for the under-sevens, and doctors and a hospital within easy reach.

For the socially-minded, life in Khartoum, especially – or if only – during the winter months, could be the greatest fun. Admittedly people tended to move in what would now be considered very restricted circles, further circumscribed in some cases by an ability or not to play bridge. The wives found the company congenial and made many long-lasting friendships quickly and easily. Familiarity did not

126

breed contempt but it did put a premium on new arrivals; many internationally interesting people passed through Khartoum after the War, and their company was pounced on and courted.

In the mornings wives met informally in each other's houses over a delicious ice-cold drink made from the abundant tiny green limes. This afforded an extremely welcome break in the otherwise interminable six-hour morning which in out-stations normally had to be spent alone. But the main time for social entertaining remained the cool of the evening, after it had become predictably and suddenly dark around six o'clock. Drinks parties held in a host's garden made a distinct improvement on the contemporaneous cocktail parties held in the U.K. in crowded noisy rooms. Apart from the meal itself, dinner parties were also held in gardens and it added greatly to the pleasure to be able to sit down on a lawn under a clear sky of stars, hearing perhaps the slight rattle of some palm fronds, or catching a waft of scent from a jasmine. The light was always agreeably subdued because any lamps, inevitably surrounded by swarming insects, had to be kept at a distance.

The pre-dinner drinking period became unduly protracted because nobody drank alcohol either at dinner or for the rest of the evening. The most usual drink offered was a finger of whisky in a pint glass of

The entrance hall of the Palace, Khartoum

water or soda. To a non-whisky-drinking wife who perhaps needed only one short drink, the wait before the meal could seem endless, especially if she had not yet acclimatised to the country and found it difficult to stay awake. For anyone else though, it remained, apart from the dawn, the best hour of the day. Sometimes the dim light (and perhaps also the whisky) encouraged comments or confidences that might otherwise never have been divulged. A degree of familiarity could be reached in an hour, which in England could have taken years of acquaintance.

After dinner, when the coffee had long since been whisked away, the host would at some point clap his hands for his *sufragi* to bring large glasses of water for everyone, the accepted *congé*. On official occasions a junior wife, however sleepy and even if she had a baby to feed, still had to wait to allow the more senior ladies to depart first.

The cooler months of December and January, two months favoured by relatives and visitors, saw a frenzied whirl of entertaining. Some went out every night of the week, often attending two functions in an evening, one of which might be the weekly dance at the club, where a wooden floor would be laid out on the lawn. But the highlight of the

Statue of Gordon (now at the Gordon Boys' School, Chobham) and tower of Khartoum Cathedral

Bridge over the Blue Nile at sunset

season was the Palace Ball, invitations to this ceremonial evening being governed by protocol. It was reminiscent of an expensive Hollywood spectacular to see the elegant couples, against floodlit palms in the Palace garden, move with slow dignity up the wide stairway before being received by the Governor-General and his wife in the lofty, pillared veranda above. The only disconcerting note was that the walls of the stairway were thickly hung with Dervish knives, guns, and other mementoes, incongruously evoking the memory of Gordon's death more or less on the same spot in 1885.

Another prestigious and enjoyable occasion in the winter was the Caledonian Ball held in the open air, usually behind the Grand Hotel. The great number of Scots in the country made this a very successful evening. Some of the remaining Sassenachs coveted an invitation but realised they would only be eligible if they could dance the reels with reasonable competence. The haggis flown in from Scotland was ceremonially piped in, and the only available drink was whisky.

No-one needed qualifications to spend an evening at 'Jimmy's' cabaret, the haunt run by a popular Syrian who did much for morale during the War. From this time, an open-air cinema showed films in

129

English, originally mainly for the benefit of H.M.Forces. The existing cinema near the station showed only Egyptian films.

As well as this professional entertainment there were two noteworthy annual amateur productions. The dramatic society had a good producer and their performances reached a high standard. The pantomimes put on at the club between 1950–56, ostensibly for the then holidaying children, proved equally entertaining, if not quite so professional.

'The idea for a Christmas pantomime came into being when a 'Gilbert' and a 'Sullivan', who had previously combined to produce a musical, found themselves both stationed together again, this time in Khartoum. Their enthusiasm spread quickly and people with talents often unsuspected by themselves became involved. Certain 'naturals' existed for some roles. Scene painters volunteered and stage constructions appeared like magic. Electricians, amateur and professional, rigged up excellent and ingenious lighting effects and concealed necessary amplifiers. Yards of gaily coloured material appeared from the market to be stitched into skirts and trousers. All this preparation had to be compressed into about three weeks so that children on their short holiday from the U.K. could participate, though rehearsals lasted only about ten days. Fortunately the weather at that time of the year was always cool and dependable. The site on the club lawn was pleasant and the Sudanese staff there enjoyed the show as much as anybody.'

One particular year proved memorable for the most elegant of principal boys, one who had only recently arrived in the country to be married to the 'Sullivan' of the enterprise. Important and delightful as she was in this temporary rôle, her chief contribution to the Khartoum community as a whole was that of a doctor.

The Cathedral Clergy House provided a year-round social centre for many Khartoum residents.

Originally, Bishop Gwynne (1863–1957), who had first come to the country with Kitchener in 1898, had been the dynamo as well as the magnet; but when he left in 1946, Archdeacon Harper, known to everyone as 'Uncle', continued the tradition. A well attended event was the simple supper in the Clergy House hall after the Sunday evening service, a custom started primarily for the Forces during the War. Numerous people, of different nationalities, became involved in the Clergy House pre-prep school, for many years the only school available for the under-sevens. These parents and their friends worked together for the massive winter bazaar held each year in aid of Cathedral and Church funds.

The Girl Guides also afforded an opportunity for international fraternising.

Ancient and modern, Blue Nile bridge

'The movement had only recently come to Khartoum and numbers were small when I became District Commissioner in 1949. Of
the three 'Blue Bird' (Brownie) flocks, one was run under the
auspices of enthusiastic teacher-nuns from the two Roman Catholic
schools and was multi-national; and the third entirely Greek. For this
flock I had to master enough of the language in order to be able to
chat to the children. The Guide and Ranger companies were also
multi-national and on our Local Association, besides Sudanese, we
had Indian, Syrian, Coptic, Greek and Italian members.

Before I left in 1955 I had helped with the adaptation of the Girl
Guide and Brownie Handbooks and their subsequent translation
into Arabic.'

Not only in Malaya did 'mad dogs and Englishmen' go out in the mid-
day sun. Many other sports could be played in the heat of the afternoon
from three-thirty onwards. Owing to great demand, the Club's tennis
courts had to be booked well in advance. The annual open tennis tour-
nament held in the winter became very popular and the finalists played
to a high standard. A few fanatics even played squash. Although by the
'fifties far fewer people kept horses, polo was still played once a week
on a bumpy sand field beyond Omdurman. Over an equally brown and

sandy area in Khartoum North certain addicts essayed a version of golf.

Perhaps the most congenial recreation in that enervating, scorching climate proved to be sailing, because, as one wife wrote, 'it was always so much cooler on the river than on land'. In 1931 the Sudan Club asked this wife's husband to arrange for four twelve-foot metal dinghies to be built in England which could later be hired out to members. 'After his leave my husband brought the plans out with him so that in the following years forty other similar boats were commissioned privately by members for their own use. On Fridays we used to race either on the Blue Nile or up at Gordon's tree on the White Nile.' Gordon's tree stood just upstream from the confluence of the two rivers, in a scrub 'forest' and marked a favourite picnic spot to which, in times gone by, Gordon is supposed frequently to have ridden.

Inexpert sailors often took their children just across the Blue Nile from the usual mooring-place outside the Club to an island opposite where they could swim or paddle in the shallow warm water. On Fridays, with a whole day available, parents often chose a longer trip up the Blue Nile to 'Crocodile' island. A sudden change of wind could make the trip uncomfortably rough for the uninitiated.

Those not interested in sailing often spent time and energy in their gardens. Khartoum's community, like any other British community the world over, had its fair number of good gardeners. Over the years they had introduced an interesting variety of flowering, often scented shrubs, and continued to experiment with different seeds and diverse plants from Kenya or South Africa. They took pride in having a display of unusual annuals rather than the ubiquitous zinnia or petunia, strikingly beautiful as these were.

Government gardeners irrigated every garden by flooding once a week, thus ensuring perpetually green lawns, a particular solace for those, living away from the river, who would otherwise have been surrounded by nothing other than gritty sand. The irrigating system rarely broke down. How this (minimal) expense for a mere amenity was ever justified in the first place is difficult to surmise; the Financial Secretary must have been a gardener himself. The flooded lawns certainly cooled the gardens temporarily, and the whole cultivated area reduced the amount of swirling dust.

Here in Khartoum, as in life anywhere else in the country, a plus could often be put against a minus.. The recipe for content lay in appreciating the one while ignoring the other, a philosophical attitude that Boswell recognised when he wrote, in an entirely different context, 'When the mind knows that it cannot help itself by struggling, it quietly and patiently submits to whatever load is put upon it.'

14 *Final Leave*

In the years after the War, several countries previously under European rule one by one gained their independence. The departure of the British Civil Service from India and that country's independence in 1947 helped to fan latent feelings of nationalism in Sudan. At first the strident public expression of these feelings was most evident among and from students and graduates of the Gordon Memorial College, which had not then been transformed into the University College of Khartoum. The fact that the College had initially been funded by private British subscriptions, following a letter to the *Times* from Lord Kitchener in 1902, had long since been forgotten. Senior members of the Political Service realised that Sudan would achieve independence in a matter of years, for which reason, after World War II, new recruits had been given contract and not pensionable terms. Few expatriates however thought the hand-over would come as quickly as it did.

There had always been *mamurs* in the Political Service and by 1950 several Sudanese Assistant District Commissioners had been promoted from that rank. It was generally supposed that when these officers had achieved the rank of Governor in the normal course of further promotion, then, and then only would the country become independent. Few people after the War could immediately accustom themselves to the ever-accelerating rate of change.

The Sudanese themselves felt divided over the type of constitution they desired. In the northern Sudan lived two religious leaders. One, Sayyid Sir Ali el-Mirghani Pasha, though ostensibly non-political, viewed favourably a union or partnership with Egypt. The other, Sayyid Sir Abd el-Rahman el-Mahdi Pasha, campaigned, and wished for no affiliation or connection with the second member of the Condominium, as he was the posthumous son of the Mahdi who in 1881 had led the rebellion against Egyptian rule. Several other smaller political parties came into existence in the years leading up to the election. The southern third of the country, administered in English, had had since slave-raiding days no love of the Arab north, and remained in general non-partisan. Life here, just as in many other out-districts well away from Khartoum, continued much as before with only a minimal awareness of current political issues.

Obviously political events in Egypt influenced feelings and attitudes in the northern part of the country and the pace of change. In 1951, for instance, Nahas Pasha, the Egyptian Prime Minister, abrogated the Condominium Treaty of 1899 and proclaimed King Farouk King of Egypt *and* Sudan. Much as this pleased some Sudanese, it stiffened the resistance of others. The dual title did not long survive, however for, after riots the following spring, the King abdicated in July 1952.

By an extraordinary coincidence General Neguib who now became President of the Egyptian Republic, had a Sudanese mother and had been to school in Khartoum. He therefore felt sympathetic to Sudan's wish for self-determination about its future status. At the same time he shrewdly stipulated a time limit of three years. In this way he won round the anti-Egyptian party who then agreed to his demand that, because he feared the influence of the British, there should be complete Sudanisation of administrative and army posts before the decision on status was taken. This upset the British who, while recognising the north's capability for self-government, had hoped for a slower hand-over, as they felt that their guidance and protection would be needed in the south.

Those wives who happened to be stationed in or around the three towns (Khartoum, Khartoum North and Omdurman) in these unsettling years found it hard to accept the antagonism of the local press. After a lifetime of easy and pleasant relationships with the Sudanese, they felt aggrieved and hurt that their husbands could be called 'bloodsucking colonial oppressors'. Had all those years of devoted care and concern been of no avail? The wives had been prepared to put up with the slings and arrows of an outrageous climate so long as it had been for a worthy cause; but once this cause had been so ungratefully denigrated, there no longer seemed any point in going on.

It is pertinent to recall some prophetic words published in 1930 by Odette Keun in her book *A foreigner looks at the Sudan:*

'No one can guess what will become of the Sudan. This fine British effort may come to destruction and nothingness. In some twenty years the essentially discordant problem of one alien race governing another may take a dangerous turn. A patriotic party may lash itself into a frenzy by the sudden discovery of wrongs and woes and will

The Legislative Assembly building, used by the Executive Council and 75 elected or nominated members from 1948 to 1952

forget every benefit derived from foreign rule. There may be, then, a withdrawal of the British from the country and if the withdrawal is premature, catastrophe and retrogression.'

Unfortunately this prediction proved to be uncannily close to the truth. After the British left, civil war smouldered between north and south for seventeen years.

During the final years of the British administration riots broke out in the three towns, as did a sudden incidence of burglaries, but security in the country as a whole seemed unaffected. Had this not been so, a wife could not have declared without any qualification at all, 'the Sudanese were a happy friendly people; I always felt entirely safe wherever I was.'

This is why the events on 1 March 1954 came as such a shock. On this day of the official opening of Parliament, the Sudanese Prime Minister had invited President Neguib down for the occasion and had, against British advice, declared the day a public holiday, which allowed large crowds of rival religious and political factions to gather first at the airport and then around the Palace. In quelling the disturbance, the unarmed British Commandant of Police and some of his force were killed. The total number of Sudanese casualties reached double figures.

135

During that summer many British officials endeavoured to find suitable professional work at home. Redundancies, commonplace today, were then almost unheard of in civilian life. What qualifications had the Political Service to offer? A knowledge of Arabic enabled a handful to be taken on by the Foreign Office. Others found their experience of local government of no practical use because the system in England appeared to be a closed hierarchy, not welcoming any outsider halfway up the scale. Significantly, the only two appointments in this field turned out to be to two 'new towns' at that time still in the process of being built. Nor did the D.C.'s legal knowledge prove an asset, being based on the Indian Penal Code which differed from English criminal law.

It became an anxious time for those with existing educational commitments at boarding schools, to which there had been no alternative while they were serving abroad. A switch to a Government day-school could not always be managed, as entry depended on passing the eleven-plus exam, not part of the prep school curriculum. Fortunately the mid-'fifties proved to be a time of expansion in the U.K. and so the majority of the Political Service had a job (or the promise of one) by the time they left Sudan. Yet no matter how congenial the new job proved, both husbands and wives had to adjust to becoming an impersonal cog in a vast machine after years serving as a known and integral part of a small enterprise. This inevitable change partly accounts for one wife's

The Sudan delegation to the Coronation, 1953. Sitt Mindamet was one of the first Sudanese women to come to England

later comment: 'I look back on my life in the Sudan with a vast amount of nostalgia. I miss all the nice friends I made there, both British and Sudanese.'

Khartoum that last winter saw a continual round of splendid if sad farewell parties. Outwardly 'the season' appeared to carry on regardless − a modern version of Nero fiddling or Drake playing bowls. The majority of the Sudanese behaved in the same way too. However vituperative their utterances in the local press, individuals retained their cheerful courtesy face to face. Many insisted on entertaining British officials for the last time and would not take 'No' for an answer. In their final fortnight many officials found themselves out for every meal of the day including breakfast.

As continuous as the farewell parties were the private auctions of household contents. At first these attracted a good attendance, but as the New Year progressed many possessions started to go for the proverbial song. Not the particular song heard on various occasions about now, which had been written by two members of the Political Service and sung to Offenbach's duet about the bold gendarmes. It was called the 'Sudanisation Blues', and many of the Service were in fact 'blues' from either Oxford or Cambridge.

We're public servants old and bleary,
We've spent a very long time here.
But now the prospect is more cheery
Because our final leave is near.
And when we think of compensation
And multiply at schedule one,
  We sack the cook,
  We start to pack
  We start to book
  Our journey back
And then we feel our duty's done.

Sometimes we feel a trifle murderous
So then we turn to schedule three
And calculate the pension third to us
And put our faith in H.M.G.
To pay the balance that is due to us
And keep the wolf pack from the door
  So home we turn
  To seek a job
  And hope to earn
  An honest bob −
Or, two or three or even more.

137

The authors were two of a group of Political Service husbands who had served in the country for around twenty years and now had to retire just before they could be made Governors. On their departure they formed a dining club of about forty members, limiting the membership to those who had been recruited between 1933 and 1939. With typical self-mockery they called themselves 'The Fallen Angels' remembering that in his book *Oriental Spotlight*, Jarvis Pasha had referred to them in 1937 as 'cock angels'. This club, which also accepted as a guest anyone who had served in the Sudan (and which after 1966 augmented its numbers by their children), has met and dined annually ever since.

Other reunions involved members from all Sudan Government departments: the annual pensioners' tea and the biennial pensioners' lunch alternating with the Sudan Church Association bazaar. Each of these events helped to nurture and preserve the unique camaraderie of a small Service. At the same time the Sudan Embassy's kind hospitality kept alive with recent news the memories of many old friends in that country. Members forged individual links with younger Sudanese when any of them happened to visit the U.K., as this following excerpt shows.

'We have just (September 1983) had Cleopatra Muhammad Negumi staying with us for three days. Her husband was an Arab merchant in Tonj just before we left in 1950, who was struck by lightning and killed when her four children were very young. We have seen a lot of her youngest, Ardil, who had been over here training as a doctor in London. He decided to fly his mother over here for a medical check-up. Cleopatra now lives in Khartoum where apparently there are no flowers any more, so she was particularly impressed by our Devon gardens. She had been back to Tonj recently and spoke most interestingly about it all. Our conversations had to be in Arabic but luckily it came back to us very quickly.'

Respect and affection for the Sudanese was genuine. Another wife wrote. 'I count it among my greatest blessings to have known these people and their country.' One possible explanation for the ease with which these relationships were made has been suggested.

'Our lasting friendship with the Sudanese has been based on sharing the same (if not particularly sophisticated) sense of humour: one not equally shared I can well imagine by many other people.'

Several wives seemed worried that they seemed to have recalled the horrendous at the expense of the normal and pleasant. Aware of this, one wrote, 'I hope I have managed to convey the happiness of my life in the Sudan and how friendly I found the people both high and low.'

Even so, when it came to the final date of departure most wives felt only too thankful to leave. The prospect of a reasonable climate, the

Sayid Isma'il El Azhari, first Prime Minister of the Sudan, seen at Fasher

end of anguished family separations, the chance to remain in one place without constant packing and unpacking, and the hope of having one real permanent home at last, together far outweighed all other considerations. The proverbial one exception proved the rule: 'When I knew we were about to leave the country for good, I cried. I was miserable at home all that first year.'

How better could the end of an era be symbolised than by the departure of a ship, which leaves a visible wake for the short period of living memory, and then disappears over the horizon and beyond the timeless waves?

'We left Port Sudan on final leave in mid-December 1954. Our ship was the Bibby liner, *Derbyshire,* due to depart at 10 p.m. We went on board in the morning and throughout the day had a constant stream of people coming to say good-bye. Our great friend, Surur Muhammad Ramli, had come to stay with us in the rest-house after we had handed over the Commissioner of Port Sudan's house to our successor, Sayyid Ali Hassan Abdulla, another friend of ours. Both of them stayed on board till the end when bottles of champagne were produced and they drank our health. Then the gangways were removed. The tugs started to pull the *Derbyshire* out from her moorings and we waved to all those still on the quayside. Suddenly all the tugs and all the ships in Port Sudan harbour began to sound their sirens. It was a most moving moment.'

Appendix I: A Live Burial in the South

In 1949 the writer's husband was District Commissioner in Tonj. This area was inhabited mainly by the Dinka tribe, who possessed religious systems of their own.

Once when we were out on trek and staying at the Athiengpuol rest-house we became involved in a midnight trek. A company of Sudan Defence Force out on manoeuvres happened to be spending the night nine miles down the road, so that evening we went down to have drinks with the two officers. At about nine o'clock a large party of Dinka, both men and women, went by making a lot of noise. We commented on it but thought no more about it at the time. Afterwards we returned to the rest house, so started our dinner later than usual.

As we were finishing our soup our houseboy, Kur, told us that our Dinka driver had told him that a man had been buried alive that day only a few miles away. So we decided to call the driver to find out more details. He reported that, when he had asked that party of Dinka where they were going, they had replied,

'We are going to a dance.'

'What - at this time of night?' he had asked.

'Ah well, not exactly a dance,' they had replied, 'more of a sacrifice.'

'What sort of sacrifice?' the driver had then enquired.

'The same sacrifice we went to this morning.' they had answered.

We were wondering what to do about this information when by chance a car drove up with Chief Akoic Majok, on his way back from the Province Council meeting in Wau. My husband asked his opinion as he was an influential chief from another area. He agreed that probably a *ban bith* (Seligman, p .198) had been buried alive. It was the accepted custom among this section of the Dinka to bury alive their religious leader and magic man as he grew old so that his spirit could pass on to his son. If he died naturally, they thought his spirit would die too. The ceremony had to be conducted secretly, as the Sudan Government ment absolutely forbade live burials.

My husband decided that he ought to investigate. So he sent for two local chiefs who had come to Athiengpuol to attend my husband's court

140

sessions. Consequently it was almost eleven o'clock before we could set off for the army camp to ask for an escort. During the journey one of the chiefs tried to persuade us that the memorial ceremony must be for a *ban bith* who had died the year before. The nine-mile journey seemed to take ages, not only because of the bumpy road but the engine also stopped three times: dirty petrol, or Dinka magic? At each stop the drums beating in the distance made us all the more impatient with the delays.

We arrived at the camp, woke up the officers and waited for an escort to assemble. At about midnight we set off. The Dinka Chief told us again that it was a very long way, but nothing daunted we started off down a very dark, narrow path. Between the eleven of us, besides the escort, we possessed only two torches, a Tilley pressure lamp and a hurricane lamp. We progressed along a horribly uneven path between two high walls of grass. Early on we met two bands of Dinka coming the other way. It was difficult to distinguish their black bodies in the dark but an array of spears gleamed in the lamplight. They were cheerful but evasive when asked whence they had come and only after persistent queries did they admit they had been at a sacrifice. Just about then the drums suddenly stopped beating.

Only half a mile farther on we came across three huts in a clearing. Two young men with spears rushed away but everything else seemed normal and three other men continued to sit innocently round their fire. The interpreter started to question them and the platoon formed up and posted scouts. I for one welcomed this precaution as nothing and no one could be seen through the high grass surrounding the huts. We all started to look around and there, sure enough, we saw a mound just beyond the light of the fire.

It stood about a metre high and more than three metres in circumference, with a pair of bull's horns on top and a lump out to one side, presumably representing the hump of a bull. A bull's severed head lay on the ground and two drums hung on a nearby tree. Beyond that we recognised some cut branches of the holy Akoic tree known to be used for the platform on which the old man lies in his grave. More branches are then put on top of him to support the bull's skin so that no earth actually touches his body. A large bowl of milk and another of beer are put beside him as he remains alive for some time. We had hoped to be in time to save the old man but the mud, still wet, had been plastered so tightly on top it seemed that anyone inside must be dead. The three Dinka admitted there had been a sacrifice but said it was only a memorial for a *ban bith* whose actual grave was a slight mound by the fire. This did not look like a grave at all, even an old one. The three Dinka looked very uneasy. My husband then asked them if he could demolish the mound to see what was inside.

141

On an order, the soldiers started digging, using broad-bladed knives to hack away the wet mud. The moon had gone behind a cloud. It was very dark and eerie. Suddenly a voice called out. For a moment I thought it had come from the mound. But it turned out to be someone in one of the huts, which only now we realised had been occupied.

Soon afterwards the soldiers had removed all the wet mud and had reached fresh dry earth. Then some branches with green leaves appeared. I felt sick. These branches must be on the old man's head and he must be standing up in a hole, I thought. We all watched fearfully, the silence broken only by the swishing of grass and a faint breathing and shuffling over to the right. Were we surrounded by a band of angry Dinka?

The soldiers paused and bent down. They had unearthed something. It turned out to be a dead goat with a string round its neck tethering it to a peg in the ground. It bore no marks nor any sign of blood, so the poor creature must have been suffocated to death. Why had this been done? No one had ever heard of this goat ceremony either before a live burial, or as a sequel. Both the chiefs were *ban biths* themselves and, although trustworthy, would not wish to interfere with age-old customs. They had probably buried their own fathers alive and would suffer the same fate themselves if their relatives were not sufficiently afraid of the Government. That night they remained loyal to their tribe and gave nothing away.

My husband apologised to the Dinka for disturbing them and promised the family a cow as compensation for spoiling their handiwork. We set off home using a different path. Within fifty yards we came to a cattle camp, the origin of the shuffling heard earlier. When we eventually reached the army camp we thanked everybody all round and climbed into our truck.

On the way back we kept pondering unanswered questions. Where had the loose earth in the mound come from? We had found no disturbed earth or hole anywhere near that clearing and Dinka do not carry earth far if they can help it. Where was the skin of that bull that had been so evidently sacrificed? Why had the two chiefs and the three Dinka by the huts been so obviously apprehensive? Where had the crowds of Dinka gone after they had passed by so noisily, earlier in the evening? Why, as the Army later told us, had the Dinka all day been carrying shields, usually a sign of a live burial? When the drums had stopped, had we been taken to the wrong place altogether? Had a warning been sent that we were coming, and had they made that atypical mound just to mislead us? We shall never know.

❋

Appendix 2: Helping out as a Doctor in Khartoum

I flew out to the Sudan on 17 November 1950, to be married in the Cathedral three days later. My husband-to-be had been a member of the Sudan Political Service for some years. I had been in General Practice in Scotland since 1943 and a clinical tutor in forensic medicine at my old medical school.

The Chief Medical Officer of Health for Khartoum, who attended our reception, lost no time in inviting me to work in the Medical Service as soon as I felt able. I was unreceptive. I now had a husband to look after, I thought, and a household to run, I thought. My stethoscope and other equipment had not yet arrived and we were about to go off for a few days' honeymoon in a sailing *dhow* along the Nile. But after our return it did not take me long to realise that my husband did not require much looking after and that our small household ran very well by itself, needing only the minimum of supervision. A long morning stretched ahead. I opened a window at the back of the house and looked out. There, in the back-yard of our house, stood the number two servant busy with the ironing. His method of dampening the bone dry cotton shirts was a surprise. He filled his mouth from a bottle of water and then, like an elephant hosing itself, sprayed it out very effectively all over the clothes. I realised that the sooner I found 'something to do' the better. So I telephoned the Chief Medical Officer and became a peripatetic Consultant.

The population of Khartoum continued to increase rapidly. The medical services, though good, were stretched. The hospitals in Khartoum and Omdurman, as in all the main towns in the Sudan, were supplemented by medical centres in outlying villages, run by medical assistants who had completed a three-year training course. This enabled them to treat everyday ailments, dispense suitable drugs and recognise anything acute, which they then passed on to the main hospital. The larger centres employed a midwife who had been trained in the Omdurman Midwife Training School and who organised ante-natal and child welfare clinics.

I had been asked to relieve the pressure on the hospital Consultant by making the medical centres even more self-contained. Each morning I visited a different centre and saw patients on whom the medical assistants wanted a second opinion. At the same time I could deal with some women with gynaecological problems.

Language remained a problem of course but I gradually picked up sufficient vocabulary to understand the gist of what was being said. Women orderlies quickly condensed long sentences spoken by the patients into a few intelligible words. Malaria and dysentery lay at the root of much ill-health, and eye troubles abounded, particularly among the children. Also babies were breast-fed for far too long, partly as an economy, so that when they eventually graduated to solids they tended to succumb to germs which caused gastro-enteritis.

We divided women with gynaecological problems into three groups: those who wanted children, those who did not want any more, and those who wanted sons rather than daughters. I remember two particularly attractive women who with their children came frequently to the clinic. They looked so much alike that I always assumed them to be sisters. This I eventually discovered not to be the case. They had the same husband, the father to both sets of children. This happy household was in no way unique.

I spent a fascinating and enjoyable year or so on this scheme which soon became well established. By then more Sudanese doctors qualified, or completed post-graduate courses abroad, so more candidates could take over my role. In response to suggestions from both Sudanese and British friends I decided to set up a private clinic in our own house. The cook's brother happened to be a good carpenter, and so he made all the required furniture for my consulting room. But instead of using the conventional white to cover the examination couch, to my surprise, he chose gaily-coloured flowers and butterflies. Cheerful and pretty, it greatly delighted the children.

When I paid his bill he asked me if I could examine his youngest son, so I made an appointment for the following morning. Though called out beforehand, I returned in plenty of time for the appointment. From my seat in the car I saw a charming tableau. The smiling, stout carpenter's wife, swathed in a spotlessly white robe, sat with her equally immaculately-dressed son on our veranda chairs, while our *sufragi* politely handed them iced fruit-juice in our best cut-glass from our silver salver. The hospitality of our house had been upheld and my practice launched with appropriate Sudanese courtesy. This proved an expensive but happy precedent.

I soon found that general practice in one country differed little from that in another. Children had measles, whooping cough, chickenpox and tonsillitis, and so sometimes did parents. People fell off horses and twisted their backs or concussed themselves. Marriages foundered, both Sudanese and British. I also treated the occasional acute appendicitis, but I never found malaria a real problem in Khartoum itself since the Public Health Administration was very good. But P.U.O. (pyrexia of unknown origin) was a frequent trial, particularly in children. No apparent cause could immediately be found except the heat and dryness. Prickly heat could of course also be troublesome and gave rise to more serious skin complaints because of its intense irritation.

In the middle of 1953 my husband was transferred out of Khartoum and I had to wind up my practice. As it happened, the move proved short-lived and within a year we found ourselves back in Khartoum again.

I sat wondering about reviving my practice when the Dean of the Kitchener School of Medicine invited me to lecture on forensic medicine to final-year students, all young men, as the first two women students were then only in their first year. They all spoke excellent English and we became good friends. They were often guests in our house and our wide-ranging discussions were wholly refreshing.

We left the Sudan in 1956 when the country became independent. I continued to practise medicine in a number of countries in the Middle East and elsewhere; but the memories of these Sudan years remain the most vivid and rewarding, principally I think because of the close friendships we made with Sudanese of all degrees. My husband worked essentially with the political leaders of the day and I should like to think that in looking after many of their families, I helped to make these relationships even closer.

In our subsequent career in the Diplomatic Service we found it a great source of pleasure to meet some of these old friends, or indeed their children, as ambassadors or other representatives of their country. We found no difficulty in starting again where we had left off , as though it had been yesterday.

✳

145

Notes on Contributors

Page numbers refer to their longer excerpts.

Acland, Bridget, (*née* Barnett), born 1902; married Brigadier P.B.E. Acland, O.B.E.,M.C., 1927; seconded to S.D.F. 1940-42, British Army 1942-45, retired S.P.S. 1946.

Two children both born U.K.; John 1928, Antony 1930. **In Sudan 1927-39; Khashm el Girba 1927-31, Port Sudan 1931-34, Geneina 1934—37, Wad Medani 1937-39. Pages 25–6, 93–5**

Aglen, Persis, (*née* Clerk Rattray), born 1916; married Edward Aglen 1939; retired as Director, Ministry of Commerce 1955.

Four children all born Khartoum; Ferelith 1948, Arminelle 1949, Brigid 1951, Francis 1955. **In Sudan 1940-55; confidential clerk Wad Medani 1940-41, Singa 1942-44 with short spell as V.A.D. in Wadi Halfa Hospital, confidential clerk El Fasher 1944-48, Khartoum 1948-55 when Girl Guide District Commissioner. Passed Sudan Government Higher Standard Arabic exam 1946. Pages 42, 66–7, 72, 75, 101, 108–9, 114, 131**

Arber, Pat, (*née* Twentmen), born 1913; married Ben Arber 1938; retired 1954 as Governor Northern Province; died 1986.

Four children; Mary born U.K. 1940, William born Khartoum 1942, Nicky born U.K. 1947, Robert born U.K. 1950. **In Sudan 1938—54; Rashad 1938-39, Khartoum 1940-44 when cipher clerk Khartoum H.Q., Kassala 1945-46, Khartoum 1946—51, Damer 1951-54. Pages 9, 38, 101–2**

Bell, Silvia, *Lady* (*née* Cornwell-Clyne), born 1919; married Sir Gawain Bell, K.C.M.G.,C.B.E., 1945; retired S.P.S. 1954 as Permanent Secretary Ministry of Interior; later Governor Northern Nigeria 1957-62.

Three children; Peta born U.K. 1946, Amanda born El Obeid 1949, Cressida born Khartoum 1954.
In Sudan 1945-54; El Obeid 1945-47, Nahud 1947-49, Cairo 1949-51, Khartoum 1951-54. Pages 10, 11, 72, 74

Blackley, Elizabeth, (*née* Deane), born 1912; married Travers Blackley, C.M.G.C.B.E., 1932; seconded S.D.F. 1940; retired S.P.S. 1949; later Chief Administrator Tripolitania (Libya); died 1982.
Six children; John born U.K. 1933, Patrick born U.K. 1936, Virginia born Canada 1944, Alexander born Tripolitania 1948, Jasper born Republic of Ireland 1952, William born Republic of Ireland 1958.
In Sudan 1932-39; Singa 1932-35, Kassala 1935-38, Gedaref 1938-39. Pages 107, 108

Blaikie, Maria (*née* Korde), born 1914; married Andrew Blaikie 1942; redundant 1954 when Commissioner Port Sudan.
One child; Jennifer born U.K. 1950.
In Sudan 1943-54; Torit 1943, Khartoum 1943-45, Khartoum North 1946-48, Singa 1948-52, Port Sudan 1952-54. Pages 67, 85, 100–1, 119–20, 139

Coriat, Kay (*née* King), born 1899 married Percy Coriat, D.C.M., M.B.E., 1926; seconded S.D.F. 1942, retired S.P.S. 1948; later Adviser to Governor, Tripolitania (Libya) 1953. He died 1960. She died 1983.
One child; Honor born U.K. 1927.
In Sudan 1927-39; Abwong 1927-31, Upper Nile Province 1933-34, Nyala and El Obeid 1936-39. Pages 16–9

Duncan, Dr Sheila (*née* Connacher), born 1920; married J.S.R. Duncan 1950; redundant 1956 when Deputy Adviser to Governor-General on Constitutional and External Affairs; later H.M. Diplomatic Service.
One child; Kirsty born U.K. 1950.
In Sudan 1950-56; Khartoum where was Assistant Medical Officer Khartoum Province, Lecturer in Forensic Medicine 1954-56, in private practice 1952-55. Page 130, Appendix 2

Haig, Rosemary , (*née* Hewett), born 1913; married John Haig 1937; redundant 1954 when Commissioner Local Courts.
Three children; Carolyn born Cairo 1943, Nigel born U.K. 1946, Andrew born U.K. 1949.
In Sudan 1938-54; Wau 1938, El Fasher 1938-40, Geteina and Dueim 1940-45, Port Sudan 1945-46, Atbara 1946-49, Khartoum 1949-54. Page 26

Kenrick, Rosemary, (*née* Tyrrell), born 1920; married John Kenrick, O.B.E., 1944; redundant 1955 when Assistant Adviser to the Governor-General on Constitutional and External Affairs.
Three children; Wynn born Khartoum 1946, Jeremy born El Obeid 1948, Penelope Jane born U.K. 1949.
In Sudan 1945-55; Talodi 1945-46, Rashad 1946-49, Omdurman 1949-53, Khartoum 1953-55. Pages 11–2, 34, 46–7, 58–9, 59 (again), 72–3, 79–80, 100, 104, 107, 109–10, 121

Lampen, Joan, (*née* Corbett), born 1915; married Dudley Lampen, C.M.G.C.B.E., 1937; retired as Governor Darfur Province 1949; died 1960.
Four children all born U.K.; John 1938, Joanna 1940, Elizabeth 1946, Mary 1948.
In Sudan 1937-49; Rufaa 1937, Rashad 1937-39, Kassala 1939-44, El Fasher 1944-49. Pages 56, 82, 106

Luce, Margaret, *Lady* (*née* Napier), born 1908; married Sir William Luce, G.B.E.K.C.M.G., 1934; retired S.P.S. as Adviser to the Governor-General on Constitutional and External Affairs in 1956; later Governor Aden Protectorate 1956-60; then Foreign Secretary's Special Representative for Gulf Affairs; died 1977.
Two children both born U.K.; Richard 1936, Diana 1939.
In Sudan 1935-39, 1945-46, 1949-56; Nyala 1935-37, Hasaheisa 1937-39, Khartoum 1945-50, Juba 1951, Wad Medani 1951-53, Khartoum 1953-56. Pages 22-3, 31–2, 33, 34, 53, 54, 60–3, 80–2, 101, 117–8
Author of plays, articles in *Punch* etc.

Mynors, Dagmar, (*née* Sjögren), born 1916; married Tom H.B. Mynors 1938; retired as Governor Blue Nile Province 1955; later Chairman East Sussex County Council 1975-77, and Chairman Sussex University Council 1980-85.
Three children; Margaret born Kenya 1941, Peter born Khartoum 1943, Charlotte born Khartoum 1946.
In Sudan 1938-55; Wad Medani 1938-39, Singa 1939-41, Wad Medani 1941-44, Khartoum 1944-53, Wad Medani 1953-55. Pages 68, 76, 84–5, 98–9, 102, 119

Oakley, Thea, (*née* Holmes), born 1901; married Arthur Oakley, O.B.E., 1926; retired 1948 as Assistant Civil Secretary (Prisons); died 1980.
Three children all born U.K.; Ann 1929, Susan 1930, John 1936.

In Sudan 1927-48; Talodi 1927-28, El Obeid 1929-34, Bahr el Ghazal Province 1934-37, Kosti 1937-43, Khartoum 1944-48. Pages 16, 21–2, 96, 111–2, 115

Paul, Elizabeth, (*née* Hooper), born 1910; married Andrew Paul 1936; retired as Governor Kassala 1955.
Three children; Elizabeth born U.K. 1938, Kerstin born U.K. 1939, Colin born Egypt 1944.
In Sudan 1936-55; El Obeid 1936-38, Dueim 1938-39 Geteina 1940, Hasaheisa 1941-45, Tokar 1947, Malakal 1949-50, Kassala 1950-55. Pages 38–9, 44, 45, 57–8, 69–70, 112–3, 120

Pawson, Peggy, (*née* Pendred), born 1922; married Philip Pawson, C.M.G., 1948; redundant 1955 when Assistant Director Local Government.
Four children; Richard born U.K. 1949, Carol born Khartoum 1950, Julia born U.K. 1954, William born U.K. 1956.
In Sudan 1948-55; Waat and Fangak 1948-49, Khartoum 1950-55. Pages 48–52, 59–60, 65, 76, 79, 82, 92, 98, 102

Robertson, Nancy, *Lady* (*née* Walker), born 1903; married Sir James Robertson, K.T., K.C.M.G., G.C.V.O., K.B.E., 1926; retired S.P.S. as Civil Secretary 1953; later Governor-General Nigeria 1955-60; died 1983.
Two children both born U.K.; James 1928, Carol 1931.
In Sudan 1926-53; Geteina 1926-27, Dueim 1927-30, Roseires 1930-33, Nahud 1933-36, Dueim 1936-39, Wad Medani 1939-41 Khartoum 1941-53. Pages 12–15, 23, 33–4, 38, 42, 42–3 (again), 63, 84, 107, 116

Simpson, Evelyn, (*née* Adams), born 1905; married Rowton Simpson, C.B.E., 1930, retired S.P.S. as Commissioner of Lands and Registrar-General 1953; later Land Tenure Adviser to Ministry Overseas Development.
Four children; Hugo born U.K. 1935, Judith born U.K. 1938, Barbara born Khartoum 1942, Lorna born U.K. 1945.
In Sudan 1930-53; Raga 1930-32, Damer 1932-33, Kajokaji 1933-36, Khartoum North 1936-40, Rhodesia 1940-41, Khartoum North 1941-43, Wad Medani 1943-44, Khartoum 1944-53. Taught at Unity High School. Pages 22, 37–8, 39–42, 66, 113, 116–7, 122

Tracey, Eileen, (*née* Bowen-Cooke), born 1904; married Christopher Tracey 1932; retired as Governor Northern Province 1948; died 1984.

Three children; Belinda born Khartoum 1935, Mary born U.K. 1937, Richard born Erkowit 1946.

In Sudan 1932-48; Khartoum and Khartoum North 1932-38, Yei 1938-40, Wad Medani 1940-43, Damer 1945-48. Pages 118, 132

Vidler, Peggy, (*née* Howard-Smith), born 1912; married Denis Vidler 1942; redundant 1955 when Commissioner of Lands. Honorary Secretary of Fallen Angels Dining Club.

Three children; Katherine born Khartoum 1944, Anne born U.K. 1946, Julia born Kenya 1948.

In Sudan 1939—54; as nursing sister Sudan Medical Service 1939-42 Atbara and Khartoum, Khartoum 1942-45, Hasaheisa 1945-49, Atbara 1949-52, Khartoum 1952-54. Pages 56, 68–9

Waugh, Daphne, (*née* Heald), born 1926; married Duncan Waugh 1950; left Sudan 1955 as District Commissioner.

Five children all born U.K.; Linda 1952, Alan 1954, Alexander 1958, Giles and Juliet 1960.

In Sudan 1950-55; Khartoum North and Khartoum.

Wilson, Anne, (*née* Alexander), born 1920; married Jack Wilson 1943; redundant 1954 when Deputy Governor Bahr el Ghazal.

Two children both born U.K. after leaving Sudan.

In Sudan 1943-54; Western Nuer District 1943-44, El Obeid 1944-45 working in Camel Corps H.Q., Tonj 1945-50, Nyala 1950-52, Wau 1952-54. Pages 35–6, 77, 89–91, 97, 98, 103–4, 110–1, 138, Appendix 1

✳

Glossary and Abbreviations

A – Arabic   D – Dinka   F – French
H – Hindi   N – Nuer   T – Turkish
U – Urdu

abray   a sweet drink based on millet (A)
A.D.C.   Assistant District Commissioner
anqarayb   locally made bed strung with rope or palm fibre twine (A)
asad   lion (A)
asl   honey (A

ban bith   a Dinka religious leader (D)
bash-katib   senior clerk (T - A)
bilharzia   parasitic disease also known as Schistosomiasis

cummerbund   sash worn round waist (U)

D.C.   District Commissioner
dhow   a term widely applied to larger Arabic vessels (A)
Dongolawi   Arabs living around Dongola
dukhn   millet (A) *Pennisetum typhoideum*
dura   grain (A) *Sorghum vulgare*

Gammexane   trade name for an insecticide – a gamma isomer of benzene hexachloride
gidal el wadi   guinea fowl (A)

habub   dust-storm, gale (A)
hafir   an area dug out to hold water (A)
hamla   the baggage train and servants of an official on trek (A)
hashish   *Cannabis sativa,* hemp. In temperate climates the fibres are used for rope; in warmer areas the top leaves develop intoxicating properties (A)

imma   turban (A)

jabal hill (A)
jallabiya a white garment like a nightshirt (A)

kanun four-legged iron frame put over a fire to take the cooking pots (A)
Keating's trade name for an insect powder
khur water course with deep sides, dry in the rainless period (A)

lau cloth knotted over one shoulder (N)
loo informal word for toilet – from l'eau (F)

malaysh never mind (A)
Mamur Egyptian or Sudanese administrative officer serving under a district commissioner (A)
markaz government post or station (A)
Mek king – (indigenous)
murasla orderly, office messenger (A)
musfah sieve (A)

namlia meat safe, derived from naml, an ant, (A). Perhaps used facetiously at first, the word soon entered common usage to describe a mosquito-wired enclosure
Nazir the chief of a tribe, given administrative and judicial powers by the Government (A)
nimitti a non-biting midge, *Tanytarsus lewisi*

oke measure of weight equivalent to 1.25 kgs, or 2.75 lbs. (The English version of the Arabic word *waqqa*.)
Omda head of a tribe, with judicial and administrative powers but subordinate to the Nazir (A)

papyrus *Cyperus nudicaulis,* floating sedge in the Sudd
piastre one hundredth part of an Egyptian pound (F)
puggaree light scarf wrapped round a sun helmet (H)
punkah a cloth-covered frame suspended from the ceiling and swung to and fro by a cord to act as a fan (H)
purdah system of secluding women from public gaze practised by Muslims (H)

qaftan caftan or kaftan, ankle-length garment with long wide sleeves (T)

ras head (A) used for cone of sugar
Reckitt's Blue trade name for a preparation which used to be used for whitening laundry

sa'at-es-sitt   your excellency the lady (A)
sawaq   driver (A)
shabura   mist (A)
Shaikh   religious or tribal leader (A)
sha'madan   candlestick with protective globe and a clever spring which automatically pushed up the candle (sha'ma) as needed (A)
sharaf   pride (A)
shufti   a look (A)
shunta   brief case (A)
sitt   lady (A)
S.P.S.   Sudan Political Service
Sudan Agent   a senior member of the S.P.S., based in Cairo or in London
Sudd   the great papyrus swamp through which the Nile makes its circuitous way for four hundred miles, from *sudd* (A), a dam
sufragi   chief domestic servant, equivalent to English butler (A)
suq   market (A)
syce   groom (H *sais*)

terai   wide brimmed, double felt hat with ventilation holes worn by white men in marshy region (Tarai) in Himalayan foothills. (H)
thawb   a long length of cloth enveloping Arabic women, often white·or indigo blue (A)
Tilley lamp   trade name for paraffin pressure lamp
tisht   bowl (A)
topi   helmet shaped hat (H) made from pith (sola in Urdu), hence sola topi
trypanosomiasis   infections caused by trypanosomes in either animals or men, one example being sleeping sickness
tukl   a round or square house, usually thatched, with walls of mud, reeds or brick (A)
tulba   a working gang (A)

V.A.D.   Voluntary Aid Detachment

wadi   valley or river bed (A)

zariba   fence of reeds or thorns making an enclosure (A)
zir   pottery jar used for storing and cooling water, similar in shape to an amphora (A)

❊

Bibliography of Books and Articles Consulted

Andrew, F.W. *The flowering plants of the Anglo-Egyptian Sudan.* T. Buncle, 1950.

Bell, *Sir* Gawain. *Shadows on the sand.* Hurst, 1983.

Beshir, Mohamed Omer. *Educational developments in the Sudan.* Benn, 1954.

Cave, F.O. *and* Macdonald, J.D. *Birds of the Sudan.* Oliver & Boyd, 1955.

Crowfoot, Grace M. *Flowering plants of the Northern and Central Sudan.* Leominster: The Orphans' Press, 1928.

Duncan, J.S.R. *The Sudan: a record of achievement.* Blackwood, 1952.

Grafftey-Smith, *Sir* Laurence. *Hands to play.* Routledge & Kegan Paul, 1975.

Henderson, K.D.D. *The making of the modern Sudan: the life and letters of Sir Douglas Newbold.* Faber & Faber, 1953.

Hillelson, S. *Sudan Arabic English-Arabic vocabulary.* McCorquodale, 1925.

Jarvis, *Major* C.H. *Oriental spotlight.* John Murray, 1937.

Keun, Odette. *A foreigner looks at the Sudan.* Faber & Faber, 1930.

Krotki, K.J. *The first population census of Sudan 1955/6.* printed by R. Kiesel, Austria, 1958.

MacMichael, *Sir* Harold. *The Anglo-Egyptian Sudan.* Faber & Faber, 1934.

MacMichael, *Sir* Harold. *The Sudan.* Benn, 1954.

Orlebar, *Colonel* John. *Tales of the Sudan Defence Force.* Privately printed, 1981.

Seligman, C.G. *and* Seligman, Brenda Z. *Pagan tribes of the Nilotic Sudan.* Routledge & Kegan Paul, 1932.

Sudan Almanac. 1955. McCorquodale & Co (Sudan) Ltd, 1955.

Wehr, Hans. *A dictionary of modern written Arabic.* Edited by J. Milton Cowan. Wiesbaden; Otto Harrassowitz, London: Allen & Unwin, 2nd printing 1966.

✳

Articles in *Sudan Notes and Records*

Acland, P.B.E. 'Notes on the camel in the Eastern Sudan.' vol. XV, part 1, 1932.

Evans-Pritchard, E.E. 'The Bongo'. vol. XII, part 1, 1929.

Lewis, *Dr* D.J. 'Nimitti and some other small annoying flies in the Sudan'. vol. XXXV, part 2, 1954.

Richards, *Captain* M.G. 'Bongo magic'. vol. XII, part 1, 1935.

Walkley, C.E.J. 'The story of Khartoum'. vol. XIX, part 1, 1936.

Willis, C.A. 'The cult of Deng'. vol. XI, 1928.

＊

Index

by Philip Ward

'Fallen Angels', 138
Fangak, 48, 79, 98
Farouk, *King*, 134
Fasher, El, 25, 72, 117, 121
Fergusson, *Captain* Vere Henry, 19
Flora, 15, 104
Furniture, 59–63

Gallabat, 39
Gambeila, 34
Gebeit, 9
Gedaref, 109
Geteina, 14–16, 29–30
Gezira Cotton Syndicate, 26–7, 58
Gordon, *General* Charles, xiv, xvi, 6, 129, 132
Grafftey-Smith, *Sir* Laurence, 3
Guides, Girl, 130–1
Gum arabic, 53
Gwek Wonding, 19
Gwynne, Ll., *Rt. Rev. Bishop*, 130

Hadendowa, 13
Haig, Douglas, *1st Earl of Bermersyde*, 3
Harper, B.J., *Rev. Canon*, 130
Hasaheisa, 39, 45
Heat, 9, 70
Home-sickness, 20
Horses and ponies, 33, 50, 95
Housing, 53–63

Independence, 133–9
Insects, 16, 51, 64–8, 127
Islamic law, 25, 30

Jarvis, *Major* C.S., 26, 138
Jebel Aulia, 14, 30
'Jimmy's' Cabaret, 129
Juba, 39, 66, 116
Jur, 19, 36, 91

Kajokaji, 116
Kassala, 26, 35, 39, 44, 67, 82, 107, 112
Keren, 43
Keun, Odette, 134
Khartoum, xvi, 6, 9–10, 12–14, 21, 28, 32, 39, 45–6, 56, 59, 64, 70–2, 87, 111–3, 116, 118–39, 143–5
Khartoum North, 14, 41, 67, 111–2, 118, 134
Khashm el Girba, 35, 93–4

Kitchener of Khartoum, Horatio Herbert, *1st Earl*, xvi, 34, 84, 123, 133
Kodok, 51
Kordofan Province, 19, 22, 104
Kosti, 26, 48

Lake Nasser, 12
Land registration, 14, 29
Land resettlement, 29–30
Languages of Sudan, 4
Latuka, 76
Laundry, 76
Limuru (Kenya), 44
Lion-hunting, 33

MacMichael, *Sir* Harold, 23
Macmillan, Harold, *Earl Stockton*, 31
Mahdi and the Mahdists, xiv, xvi, 134
Malakal, 16, 29, 48–51, 87, 97, 116
Marriage, 21–5
Marsa Barghout, 6
Mayall, R.C., 4
Medical services, 143–5
Mombasa (Kenya), 39

Nahas Pasha, 134
Nahud, 19, 116
Namasagali (Uganda), 39
Nannies, 37–9, 41–2, 115–6
Neguib, *President* Muhammad, 134–5
Negumi, Cleopatra Muhammad, 138
Nile, 11–12. *See also* Blue Nile, Upper Nile Province, White Nile
Nuba, 106
Nuba mountains, 16, 96
Nuer, 16, 19, 51, 82, 92
Nyala, 32–3, 93, 110, 117–8

Obeid, El, 26, 32, 72, 96, 107, 116, 118
Omdurman, xvi, 107, 114, 134, 143
Opari, 66
Orlebar, *Col.* John, 3

Polo, 23, 26–8, 33, 118, 131
Port Sudan, 6, 9, 13, 21, 85, 87, 119, 139

Raga, 22, 116
Rahad, 93, 121
Rail travel, 6, 9–11, 13, 48

❋

OLEANDER TRAVEL BOOKS

LIBYA PAST AND PRESENT

ARABIA PAST AND PRESENT

ANNALS OF OMAN
Sirhan ibn Sirhan

ARABIA IN EARLY MAPS
G.R. Tibbetts

ARABIAN GULF INTELLIGENCE
comp. R.H. Thomas

**ARABIAN PERSONALITIES OF THE
EARLY TWENTIETH CENTURY**
introd. R.L. Bidwell

DIARY OF A JOURNEY ACROSS ARABIA
G.F. Sadleir

THE GOLD-MINES OF MIDIAN
Richard Burton

HA'IL: OASIS CITY OF SAUDI ARABIA
Philip Ward

HEJAZ BEFORE WORLD WAR I
D.G. Hogarth

HISTORY OF SEYD SAID
Vincenzo Maurizi

KING HUSAIN & THE KINGDOM OF HEJAZ
Randall Baker

THE LAND OF MIDIAN (REVISITED)
Richard Burton

MONUMENTS OF SOUTH ARABIA
Brian Doe

OMANI PROVERBS
A.S.G. Jayakar

SOJOURN WITH THE GRAND SHARIF OF MAKKAH
Charles Didier

TRAVELS IN ARABIA (1845 & 1848)
Yrjö Wallin

TRAVELS IN OMAN
Philip Ward